Sea of
Heartbreak

Sea of Heartbreak

An Extraordinary Account of a Newfoundland Fishing Voyage

Michael J. Dwyer

With a Foreword by Farley Mowat

KEY PORTER BOOKS

Canadian Cataloguing in Publication Data

Dwyer, Michael, 1953–
    Sea of heartbreak: an extraordinary account of a Newfoundland fishing voyage

ISBN 1-55263-303-9

1. Dwyer, Michael, 1953–   .   .   2. Styx (Trawler).   3. Fisheries – Newfoundland.
4. Turbot industry – Newfoundland.   I. Title.

SH224.N7D89 2001   639.2'2'09718   C2001-930171-5

The publisher gratefully acknowledges the support of the Canada Council for the Arts and the Ontario Arts Council for its publishing program.

We acknowledge the financial support of the Government of Canada through the Book Publishing Industry Development Program (BPIDP) for our publishing activities.

Key Porter Books Limited
70 The Esplanade
Toronto, Ontario
Canada M5E 1R2

www.keyporter.com

Electronic formatting: Jean Lightfoot Peters
Design: Peter Maher
Map and diagram drawn by John Lightfoot

Printed and bound in Canada

01 02 03 04 05 06 6 5 4 3 2 1

This book is dedicated to the creatures mentioned within.

Acknowledgments

I HUMBLY ACKNOWLEDGE THE HELP received from my family and friends. A special thank you to my sister, Anita, and my daughter, Michelle.

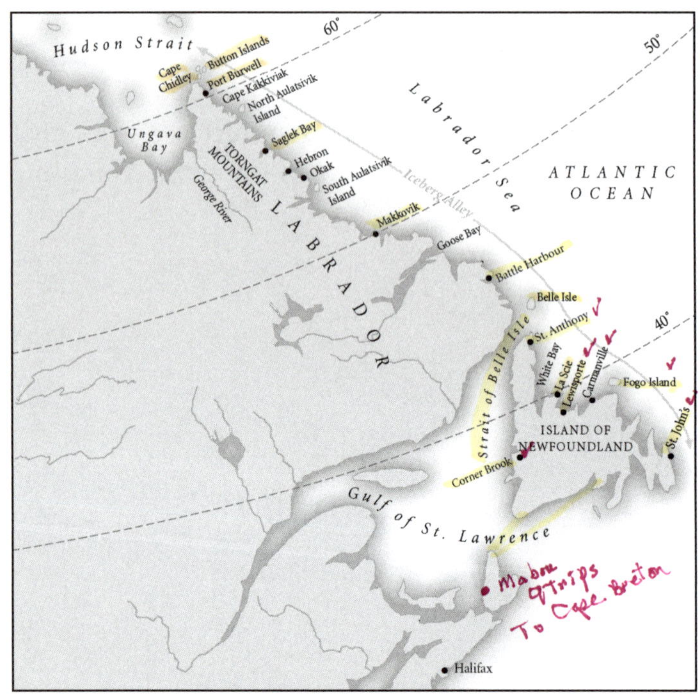

Newfoundland and Labrador, the northeastern coast.

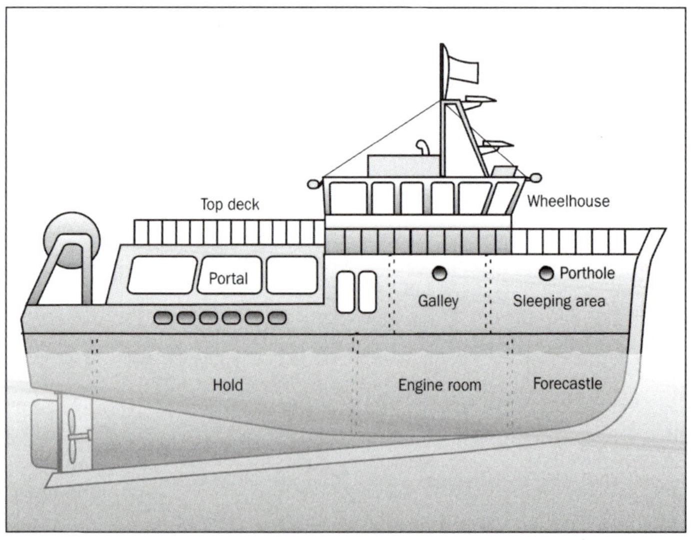

A typical 65-foot fishing vessel.

Foreword

THE DEGRADATION AND DESTRUCTION of the animate world by human beings goes on apace. The effect of this mayhem on the land has long been apparent, but what has been happening on the sea has been mostly concealed from view. Only within the past several decades has the magnitude of the bloodletting in the oceans become obvious.

The massacre of the whales gave us our first major indication of the extent of the damage we were wreaking on marine life. What we did to the whales was terrible enough, but what we have done to the seals, and especially to the ice seals of the North Atlantic, constitutes an atrocity of such dimensions that it boggles the mind.

In the winter of 1998 I sent a letter condemning the seal slaughter to every major newspaper and magazine in Canada. Some of them published it. Here are a few excerpts:

By lavishly subsidizing hunters; by saturating the media with misinformation; by ignoring or perverting scientific data, politicians and the fishing industry seek to justify an ongoing massacre of harp and hood seals which is officially recognized as amounting to a quarter of a million animals each year. However, the actual kill, including seals wounded but not recovered, mounts to a veritable holocaust of something between half a million and a million animals.

The only significant monetary return from this massive shedding of blood comes from the sale of seal penises in Asia, where they are used to make aphrodisiacs.

As of 2001 the governments of Canada and of Newfoundland continue to promote and subsidize this, the most notorious, the largest and the most outrageous annual butchery of wild mammals taking place anywhere on earth.

Only in Canada?

Only in Canada!

That is by no means the worst of it. In recent years we have witnessed, with incredulity, the implosion of the age-old myth that there are more fish in the sea than have ever come out of it. The fact is that the numbers of the top 100 food-fish species (food for us) in the world's oceans have been so drastically reduced (by us) that more than 70 percent are now listed as being "economically threatened" (which means they are now so scarce as to be hardly worth hunting); while almost half the species of prime food-fish are threatened with the possibility, or even likelihood, of literal extinction.

And yet…and yet…still we refuse to accept the genocidal reality of what we are doing to the living world. We refuse to change our ways. We ignore the dire warning of previous slaughters and heedlessly continue on our course as the most destructive animal ever to have afflicted this planet.

The ongoing wastage of life in the sea is vehemently justified and defended by politicians and by vested economic interests, supported by hired-gun scientists working for both. One of the arguments raised in justification of continuing the slaughter is that the "fishery" (whether for whales, seals or fishes) is not only economically, but is culturally vital to the survival of fishermen. We are told that to stop the massacre, or to seriously curtail it, would result in depriving fishermen of a precious and vital part of their own, and the overall human heritage.

The image of the fisherman as an enduring, and endearingly rough-hewn fellow of sterling virtues, who kills fish and seals (compassionately) only to make an honest living for his family, has been deeply imprinted. I admit that, in some of my own writings, I have had a hand in creating this image.

However there is another aspect to the portrait—one that the propagandists for the fishery have not brought under public scrutiny. This is the reality of what and who the fisherman really is and what he does.

Michael Dwyer is a Newfoundland fisherman and sealer. Not only is he a singularly straightforward and observant man, he is also a remarkably courageous one for he has done what no other commercial fisherman in Atlantic Canada has dared to do. He has written a book that, in his own succinct and pungent words, describes what actually happens in this traditional cultural activity, and how it shapes the psyche and the lives of those who are engaged in it.

Sea of Heartbreak may not be to everyone's taste, but it is absolutely *de rigueur* for anyone seeking to understand the why and the wherefore of one of the mainsprings of human behavior, and for all who dare to face the truth about the nature of our kind.

—Farley Mowat

Sea of
Heartbreak

Tuesday, August 25

WHEN THE PHONE RANG THAT MORNING, I was in desperate need of a job. For reasons and circumstances beyond my
control, I had degenerated over the course of the last fourteen
years from being a productive member of a happy household to
being a mostly unhappy, near income-less, middle-aged
dependent whose wife kept the wolves at bay.

Those were the darkest, most depressing, stressful, demoralizing days of my life. The hardest times for me came at the start
of my wife, Beulah's, workday. When she threw off the covers to
get ready for work, a blanket of shame would cloak me entirely.
I'd lie in bed and listen as she sped away and the shame would
stay with me all day.

My unemployment caused tension between my wife and
me. Our marriage was nearly on the rocks. Our sex life had all

but died. At one time it had been an anywhere at anytime sort of sex life. Nowadays, mostly we practiced "hall sex." When we met each other in the hallway, we'd exchange the finger sign. As is always the case in situations like ours, everyone suffers.

I had to get a job. Everything hinged on it. There was no job for me here on the island. Out-migration was the only way. There were three options available to us. Plan A: Go solo. I would head out west to find work as a trucker. Beulah would stay and hold the fort.

To be honest, I harbored a few qualms about that option. It is not easy to be away from home, alone, in a strange city dealing with the stresses and uncertainties that come with a new job—paperwork, maneuvering massive b-trains (the big-rig combination of tractor, lead trailer and pup), strange superhighways, trying to find exits, rushing to make sched- ules, struggling to survive, paying through the nose every run of the way, all the while supporting and maintaining a family far away.

Besides, I was aware that my two kids were at critical ages. They needed the guidance, discipline and assurance that a father brings. No father looks forward to leaving behind all that means anything. Wolves wait, intent upon nothing but blowing asunder what one has built. Men have returned after only a short time to find an abandoned pile of rubble where once stood the fort.

Plan B was to sell everything we owned, rent a U-Haul and, together, leave Newfoundland. The downside here was the fact that even if we were lucky enough to sell the house and prop- erty, the money received would not be nearly enough for a down payment on a home in Calgary. Between the two of us, sixty years of struggle, investment, dreams and tender loving care didn't add up to a down payment. That realization alone was enough to take the wind out of our sails.

And if we couldn't sell the house, would we rent it out to cover the mortgage? Who would we rent to? Who would care for our things? What would be left of the place upon our return? Would we ever return?

We could leave the house vacant. Drain the water, board up the windows and desert the place. Leave the key with somebody to keep an eye on things. That meant a mortgage payment, a heating bill and repair bills here in Newfoundland and an even higher cost of living in Calgary. We'd need to buy a car. Depending on the work we found, maybe two cars.

What about Mark and Michelle? What about our aging parents? Would we ever see them alive again? What about our families? Friends? What would happen to our old hound dog, Gunner?

Also, as a patriot of this beautiful island province of Newfoundland, it concerned me that if everyone chose or was forced to leave here, there would be no one to protect what we cherish and hold dear from those who are waiting to prey on what little we have left.

But I needed an income. The time was nigh. I had to choose. What's it going be, boy? What's it going to be?

~~~~~~

A voice on the other end said, "Mick, this is Wayne. We're going north to Ungava Bay for seven or eight weeks fishing turbot. We pay 6 percent. Do you want to come along?"

My response was immediate and spontaneous and would have been the same if he had said that they were going to Cairo for a load of camel dung. Plan C had presented itself. Six percent of something is a lot better than one hundred percent of nothing. "Wayne, you don't have to look any further. When do we leave?"

"The *Styx* is tied up in Wesleyville. We'll be ready to sail around dinnertime tomorrow," he replied in a happy-to-have-you-aboard tone of voice.
~~~~~~

I didn't exactly know what turbot fishing involved other than the fact that turbot was fished in deep water using gill nets, usually far offshore. To say the least, I was a man of limited fishing experience.

My father, Leo, was a seafarer, not a fisherman. There was a short time that he was at home and together we set out a few gill nets to catch cod. That was in the time when every Newfoundlander had a right to take from the sea as a farmer takes from the fields.

The gillnetting operation was on a small scale. Using an eighteen-foot speedboat, we would tie five gill nets together and set them out on a prime fishing ground in the bay. Each morning for a week, dawn would find us speeding towards our gear, which we'd pull from the bottom manually. We didn't catch a lot of cod, but we did catch a lot of sea creatures. When I mentioned the efficiency of the nets in regards to entangling sea creatures, my father said, "My son, gill nets are going to be the ruination of the ocean. You mark my words. They should never be allowed to be set." At week's end Dad received a call to go away and we took up our gear. I had never set another gill net since.

"Wayne, is there anything special that I will need to bring along?" I asked, suspecting that there were no department stores where we were going.

"No, nothing special," he replied. "Bring lots of clothes and a warm sleeping bag because you have to sleep in the wheelhouse. Bring a spare pair of rubber clothes along, and you will need gloves. You can buy them tomorrow at the store in Wesleyville where we buy supplies for the ship."

"Okay, Wayne, thanks for calling. I'll be ready."

"Oh yes, I almost forgot. You will have to go to DFO and buy a temporary fishing permit. That costs fifty dollars," he added casually. "Make sure you do that today because I'll be picking you up around seven tomorrow morning."

"Okay, Wayne, I'll do that, and I'll see you in the morning."

It made Beulah's day when at dinnertime she came home and I told her about Wayne's call and the voyage to Ungava Bay. The kids were elated that dad finally had a job. I was uplifted as well. When I am working my demeanor is light-hearted, my self-esteem runs high and it reflects on my family. When I am dead in the water, I am not a nice fellow to be around.

The rest of the day was spent in a flurry of activity getting ready for the voyage that saw me spend close to four hundred dollars. Beulah, my minister of finance, came up with the necessary money from somewhere.

We thought it to be a good investment. With the fishery in the sad state that it is in, if one has to wet one's feet and get into the fishery, the larger draggers, such as the *Styx*, were the place to be. Being bigger, the vessels were more comfortable, could carry more supplies that enabled them to stay out longer, fish farther offshore, set more gear, survive stormy seas and make bigger catches, thereby making more money for companies, captains and crews alike.

Wayne was not a lifelong friend of the family. Actually, I hardly knew him. He was, at forty-five, the youngest of three brothers who had moved to our once vibrant seaport town of Lewisporte in the last year.

The brothers were of a fundamental religious family who had invested in the fishery over the past few years. Among them they now owned two offshore fishing boats—the MV *Styx* and the MV *Vantage*. They had each bought a large house in the moneyed part of town, with hardly sufficient acreage to accomodate their full-sized, late-model cars, pickups, quad-runners, snow machines and fifth-wheel trailers.

Wayne served as first hand on the *Styx*, commanded by the oldest brother, Ben, who was about fifty years old. The *Styx* usually carried a contingent of six crewmembers, including Ben's son, Greg.

I assumed that the reason Wayne called me about the voyage was because the third brother, Jerry, had told him that I was a good candidate for the job. He knew firsthand that I worked like a dog under the most grueling of conditions for little or no pay—exactly the kind of man he was looking for.

The *Vantage* was an older, smaller vessel than the *Styx*, with an overall length of just sixty feet. The *Vantage* would be accompanying us on the voyage to Ungava. Made of wood recently fiberglassed over, she was commanded by Jerry and crewed by seven men, including Jerry's son, Rodney. I had gone to the Newfoundland seal hunt in the ice fields off the northeast coast on the *Vantage* the previous spring.

At that time, it had been a long time since I had been out to the hunt and I had forgotten how gruesome and dangerous the work was. And I had forgotten how meager sealers' earnings were. One day we were in what seemed to be the very heart of the harp nation. Seals were coming in on all sides and almost everyone was slaving in the blood, grease and bitter cold. It was during one of those infrequent times when I stopped to eat that Jerry came to the galley. Standing in the doorway, he said, "I got to say, Mickey, that you are as good as any two men, no, any three men, that ever worked on this boat." Before I could get a chance to respond, he was gone.

I didn't make much money that spring, but it seemed I left an impression that they could capitalize on.

Not that I was complaining. I practically had my foot in the door for a good-paying job that would mean no longer having to face the tortures, torments, trials, tribulations and uncertainties of having to uproot my family and move away. In a matter of hours, I was going away, back to sea, north to Ungava Bay.

At midnight my bags were packed. I was ready to go.

Wednesday, August 26

I WAS READY AND WAITING WHEN WAYNE pulled into the driveway shortly before 8 a.m. in a pickup truck loaded with gear. Bags of monofilament gill nets and a crab pot filled with coiled rope, coolers, boxes and luggage took up most of the room. After some rearranging, room was found to stow my gear. A few fleeting kisses, hugs and good-luck wishes and we were on our way to the *Styx*, which was tied up to the government wharf in Wesleyville.

Wayne was only about five feet tall. His square head seemed too large for his stout, muscular body. But he seemed fit as a fiddle and was all smiles as he eased the transmission into high and the V-8 engine planed off in scrabbling gear.

Quite abruptly and for no apparent reason, Wayne applied the brake and said, "You never brought your gun."

"I didn't think I'd need it," I replied.

"You didn't bring a fishing rod, either?"

"No, I never thought of it."

"It don't make any difference. There will be plenty of rods and guns aboard. The boys are bringing theirs."

As the miles sped by Wayne did most of the talking, informing me that it was a little late in the year to be going north. Apparently, the lure was the fact that for the first time in history, Ungava Bay was being opened up for commercial fishing. A turbot quota was to be set and the thought of new, virgin fishing grounds was too big a bait to resist. The traditional fishing grounds were not as productive as they once were. In fact, they were at the point of being fished out.

Wayne also talked exuberantly and in great length about the wildlife of Labrador, particularly the geese, ducks, arctic char and caribou. He asked me if the Lewisporte area was a good place to shoot moose. When not talking, he hummed or sang some hymn or another.

I listened to what he had to say, fought hard to stifle yawns and contributed a few words now and again. Mostly, I thought of what I could possibly have forgotten to take along, and I dealt with the stresses that come with starting a new job with a new crew onboard a strange ship atop an often violent ocean.

~~~~~~

The *Styx* was a beehive of activity when Wayne stopped the truck on the wharf. Final preparations were being made for the voyage. With little time taken for introductions, the crew swarmed the truck and in jig time the gear we carried was stowed. Greg was to go to the store in the truck to get more supplies. It was a chance for me to get the gloves I needed. "Greg, I'm coming along with you," I said.

"Jump aboard," he replied.

Greg was Ben's only son. He was twenty-five—tall and slim, over six feet tall and weighing about one hundred and fifty pounds. Everything about him seemed wild, especially the glint in his eyes and the mop of seemingly untamable, jet-black hair. His driving habits spoke volumes as the accelerator struck the floor and the tires screeched.

Thankfully, the store wasn't that far away and the rally ride only lasted a few minutes. Inside the store, Greg and the female clerk went about filling the order and loading it in the truck. A male clerk with pearly-white teeth, who I assumed was the owner of the store, approached me and asked, "Can I help you, sir?"

"Yes, sir, you can," I replied. "I'm going fishing onboard the *Styx* and I'll be needing some gloves."

"How many pairs do you need?" he asked in a friendly tone.

I wasn't sure, so I asked Greg. "Well, it's hard to say," he
~~~~~~

replied. "If the fish is plentiful, they don't last very long. If the garbage is plentiful, they wear out even quicker. We wear two pairs at a time, a pair of cotton over a pair of rubber. I'd say you'll need five dozen pairs of each."

"What do you mean, 'garbage'?" I asked.

"Garbage is anything that comes in over the side that we don't ice down in the hold. On this voyage, anything but number one turbot is garbage," he replied.

To see the big box of gloves surprised me. I was even more surprised and taken aback when the clerk totaled the bill at one hundred and thirty dollars. Previous experience told me that whenever or wherever one travels, even to the desolate shores of northern Labrador, one must carry some cash. With only one hundred and twenty dollars to my name, I didn't want to go broke. Knowing that in all small outports the general store carries charge accounts, I inquired of the clerk, "Can I pay one hundred dollars on the bill now and pay the remainder when I get back?"

With what I took to be a smile of sincerity, he replied, "Yes, sir, no problem."

I pressed the bargain and said, "God forbid, but in the event that we do not get a lot of fish or garbage and I don't use a portion of these gloves, can I return them and put the money towards the bill?"

Without changing a facial feature, he replied, "Yes, you can, so long as the gloves are in the original wrapping."

"Okay, thank you. One hundred dollars I will pay." Time would tell that he was lying through those pearly-whites. He reneged on the promise; Beulah paid the bill.

Two more crewmembers, Hector and Todd, arrived in a pickup and soon both trucks were loaded with boxes, bags, buckets, cartons and cases of food. Hector, a big brute of a man who reminded me of the Hulk, handled the fifty-pound buckets as if they were empty. His most outstanding feature next to sheer bulk and strength was a quick and friendly smile that often lit up his bearded face. He seemed to be easygoing and good natured and I took a liking to him right away. He had worked as share man on the *Styx* for the past six years.

Todd had the same body type as Wayne but was taller. He had married Ben's daughter five years ago and had worked on the *Styx* ever since. My first impressions of him were favorable. He appeared friendly and eager to talk as he worked. Already there were beads of sweat breaking out on his forehead from the labor of loading.

By four in the afternoon, with the trucks parked in a friend's yard for safekeeping, we slipped the lines and set sail for Ungava Bay, over nine hundred nautical miles away.

My first order of duty after we got under way was to find somewhere to put my gear. The *Styx* was sixty-five feet overall and twenty-four feet wide and was built in standard dragger fashion. The hull was painted blue; the low-profile, forward superstructure was white. There were three decks. The top deck was where the wheelhouse and aft top deck were located. The main deck housed the galley, head and crew sleeping quarters and the aft shelter deck. The basement was home for the four-hundred-and-fifty-horsepower Caterpillar diesel engine and the holding space for fuel, water and one hundred thousand pounds of fish.

The three brothers had purchased the *Styx* new from the shipyard eight years ago and had spared no expense outfitting her for the fishery. Like the *Vantage*, she was equipped with the latest in electronic and navigational devices that aided in the seeking and catching of fish. The shelter deck was set up like a mini-fish plant with the gurdy, the stainless steel picking table, the holding tanks and the gutting table taking up most of the room.

Down in the engine room Don, the engineer, helped me find room for my outside clothing. Don was about my age and the smallest man aboard next to me. He seemed quite at home amid the heat, the fumes and the noise that the main engine made. Before we found room for the box of gloves I had with me, there was sweat streaking down our faces.

With my sleeping gear and clothes bag, I headed up the steep, steel steps and onto the spacious bridge. Ben sat in the commander's chair on the starboard side. Behind the chair and against the wall was a bench covered in black vinyl. My heart sank a little when I realized that it was to be my bed. I had slept on benches before and the experiences had not been pleasant. I placed my bags on it and sat down. It was, as expected, hard as a rock.

Other than that, things were great. I harbored good feelings about the crew and as the *Styx* cleared the farewell buoy and rose to meet the first gentle swells of the open sea, I had a building sense of reassurance in her. Under my feet the hull vibrated, feeling solid and capable of doing a fully satisfactory job of getting us to the fishing grounds and back in one piece.

I had seafaring experience enough to know that a sixty-five-foot vessel was, at the best of times, not very big atop the North Atlantic Ocean. For that matter, a ship three hundred and fifty feet long was not very big on the high seas at times. Survival and success ultimately weighed on the captain's shoulders and the engineer's abilities to keep the engine going. At sea, conditions deteriorate quickly. At times it's second by second survival. The success of the voyage depended on decisions made about the weather and the tides, the coordinates and the depth of water. It was plain to see that, in the past anyway, the brothers three had made good decisions and I had no qualms about their competence.

By six o'clock I was all settled in. Most everyone congregated in the galley to eat the pork chops that Jack had cooked. The small space was steaming hot and congested as seven burly men prepared to eat. A television set with VCR was mounted on the wall above the deep freezer. A videocassette of a church choir provided background music.

Todd, holding a plate piled high with steaming food drenched in gravy, maneuvered his way through the mayhem to report to the bridge to watch "Otto," the autopilot, maintain course.

"Grab a plate, Mickey, pick up some grub and take a seat," Jack said, with sweat on his crimson face and steam on his glasses. "Eat hardy, my son. There's more fat on Good Friday than there is on you. We're going to have to fatten you up."

Jack was thirty-five years old and doubled as the onboard cook. Second in size only to Hector, Jack had worked on the *Styx* for seven years. He was married to another of Ben's daughters and had two small children. With captain's credentials, Jack commanded the *Styx* when Ben stayed ashore. He seemed friendly and from the smell and looks of things, he was a good cook.

"A few pounds wouldn't hurt for sure," I replied with a laugh, standing to one side as Hector swayed by with a feast and sat at the small table that was covered with a blue rubber-backed tablecloth and set with paper towels. Buffet style, I chose my supper and slid in next to him.

There wasn't much room to spare after all had taken their places on the two facing benches. For a short while the only sounds were the singing of the tabernacle choir, the steady throb of the main engine, the sounds of water washing along the hull and the hubbub a hungry fishing crew makes when eating a mountain of food. I felt right at home. Soon, plates were bare and bowls empty and there seemed a lot less space at the table.

Ben sat with what must have been only one cheek on the seat at the end of the bench facing Hector, Don and I. With a loud burp, he wiped away sweat with a paper towel and threw it on the empty plate. "Well, boys, we're on our way to Ungava Bay. What do you say?"

Greg, who was separated from Ben by Jack, was first to rise for the fly. "I think it's an awful long ways to go to catch turbot. By the time we get down there and back, we could have made three trips to the grounds off Wesleyville. It don't make sense to me."

"Yes, that might be true," Ben replied. "It's a gamble. But that's the way of the fishing game. We don't know what's down in Ungava Bay. The waters have never been fished before. It's the same now as when Hudson found it. It's virgin waters. The bottom might be carpeted with great big turbot."

Wayne interjected with a gleam in his eye, "Wouldn't that be something, eh? A big fat turbot in every mesh. You never know until you try, do you, boy?"

"We might not get to find out," said Greg. "They might not even open the bay for turbot fishing. We're only going down there on speculation. What do we do in the meantime?"

"Speculation. It's all speculation. You got to speculate to accumulate, my son," Ben stated in a voice spiked with piss and vinegar. Leaning forward, he said, "Until the season in Ungava Bay opens, we fish the waters of the Labrador Sea. They say the weather is generally good up there in the fall of the year. With the Good Lord willing, we might have a good trip made of it before they open Ungava Bay and the turbot we catch there will be icing on the cake."

Greg was about to rebut, but Jack cut him off. "You know as well as I do what the grounds off Wesleyville are like. We've been fishing them for years and each year we have to work a lot harder and longer for smaller and smaller catches. Those grounds are picked clean. I say it's the right thing to do. Where's your sense of adventure?"

"Sure, boy," Ben added, picking food from his teeth with a toothpick. "Where's your sense of adventure? To boldly go where you have not gone before? To seek out new fishing grounds and make a barrel of money?"

"I don't know about a barrel of money," Greg replied dubiously.

Quietly and contentedly, I sipped tea and watched and listened to what crews do and talk about while at sea. Through the din, the figure of fifteen thousand dollars came to my ears. That excited me. Through the opened porthole, refreshing salt air wafted in. The acquatic horizon rose and fell with the gentle listing of the hull.

"Well, we'll know a lot more about turbot fishing in the Labrador Sea and Ungava Bay in a couple of months' time," Ben stated as if to end the conversation. Abruptly, he arose from the table and disappeared into the washroom. The space was quickly gobbled up, and then, it seemed, the choir held everyone's attention.

The grinding of the toilet motor signalled that it was time to move out. "What are you going to do, Mick, wash or dry?" Hector asked, making the motion for me to follow Don.

"Wash," I replied, shifting to take up position at the sink. The crew dispersed, some to their rooms, others to the bridge.

Hector began to clear the table by placing the cutlery in a bowl. The bottles of pickles and beets, the sugar basin, and the milk and jam he put in their slots in the wooden holder bolted to the bulkhead below the porthole. The empty bottles, cans, Styrofoam plates and cups and other refuse he tossed out through the porthole. The garbage that couldn't go through the porthole was compressed into a green plastic bag. All the while, he sang along with the choir in his Sunday-go-to-meeting voice.

The open porthole over the sink reminded me of a small TV screen with seagulls fluttering and squawking in living color.

Supper was served. By the time the galley was cleared away, dishes washed and put away, countertop and rubber tablecloth cleaned, the stove shining again, the floor swept and mopped, I craved caffeine, nicotine and a wide-open space. As I was making my way outside to the shelter deck, Hector said, "Toss that garbage over the side when you go out."

Grabbing the green plastic bag, I took it to the stern. At a glance, I could tell that we were in for a spectacular sunset and a nice day tomorrow; "Red sky at night, sailor's delight." It was as nice as it could possibly get at sea.

Following orders, I tossed the garbage bag over the side. Three or four seagulls that trailed the wake braked and wheeled to investigate, but none pitched. Watching the bag fall astern, playing peekaboo in the swells, I tried to remember the last time I had done such a shameful thing as to deliberately pollute the sea with garbage. Out of the blue, just before the bag was forever lost from my view, my memory served me. It had been seal hunting on the *Vantage*.

As with any sea voyage, in preparation for the seal hunt, we had loaded truckloads of supplies onboard the *Vantage*. We may have brought two bags of garbage back to shore. The rest went out the porthole or over the side. Such was the way of some fishermen, I guessed.

Scanning the tranquil aquarium, I saw no sign of any other ship. The *Vantage* had prepared for the voyage at La Scie. They would join up with us later.

~~~~~~

It felt good to be working again. I'd been getting the odd plumbing job. Then, there'd be dry spells when a month or more would go by and I didn't do a tap. With bill collectors hounding me, I was on the verge of a nervous breakdown.

"It's better to be at this," I said aloud to an inquisitive seagull
~~~~~~

that effortlessly kept pace mere feet from me, although I did not exactly know what "this" was. All I was sure of was that I was heading north at a speed of 8.5 knots with the setting sun trying to burn the last of summer into my face.

The thought of earning fifteen thousand dollars and maybe a chance to become part of the crew on this ship or some other lifted my spirits. Dragger crews usually made more than eighty thousand dollars a season. What I could do with that kind of income. The sounds of the water along the hull seemed to say, "The worst is over. Your ship has finally come in." A seagull clucked confirmation as it glided by.

The lights were shining through every window on the bridge when I went inside a short while later. Ben sat up in the commander's chair, picking his teeth with a toothpick. Greg was standing before the chart table plotting our position. "Beautiful evening out there now, skipper," I said, sitting in the portside rumble seat behind Greg.

"Yes, it is, isn't it," Ben replied, swiveling the chair towards me. "It don't get much nicer than this out here."

Using a pair of dividers, Greg plotted the coordinates displayed on the Global Positioning System onto a chart showing White Bay and a portion of the Great Northern Peninsula. Satisfied with the reckoning, he turned out the lights. The bridge was suddenly flooded with the soft lights of the instruments and the afterglow of the sunset. No one spoke.

As I sat there my weight shifted with the swell on the vinyl seat covering. Distinctly, the material squeaked under one cheek before my weight shifted to the other, making another squeak. One complete cycle, squeak to squeak, cheek to cheek, every eight seconds.

The evening star flickered on and before long the Big Dipper was emptying a splash of stars into the night sky. All in all it made for what my father would classify as "a great time along."

About then, the searchlight mounted atop the wheelhouse flared on to light our course through the night. In the added glow, I discerned the bench and my rolled up sleeping bag in the corner. I felt drained and exhausted. Reluctantly, I made a move to make its acquaintance.

Ben and Greg seemed not to notice me making my bed and peeling off my outer clothes. Lying on the bench with my pillow under the windows against the starboard bulkhead, with my feet pointing to port, I soon found the bench to be, as I feared, no different than all the other benches I had known—hard and uncomfortable. Stretching out completely, my toes barely touched the far end. To my open right side, there was less than a foot to spare. Lying on my back, I closed my eyes.

"*Vantage. Vantage. Vantage.* This is the *Styx.* Do you read? Over." Ben was hailing the *Vantage* on the radio.

Loud and clear, Jerry's tinny voice filled the bridge. "*Styx, Styx,* this is the *Vantage.* Twenty-one-eighty two, Ben."

"Roger." Ben clicked through the channels. "You read, Jerry?"

"Yes, boy, got you loud and clear. What's your coordinate? Over."

The lights glared on and Greg plotted the *Vantage*'s position as Ben relayed our coordinates so they could plot us.

"They're about twenty-two miles south-southwest of us," Greg reported after a spell working with the dividers.

Ben moved from the chair to check, stretching the cord of the mike. "Yeah, Jerry. You're twenty-two miles south-southwest of us. What's your speed? Over."

"Eight point two knots. Over."

"Back. I see, boy. Yeah, we're doing 8.5 knots. I'm going to slow her in a little." Ben reduced the Cat's fuel feed and I could distinctly feel the change in vibration and thrust of the hull. "We're slowing to five knots. At this rate, we should be in company before dawn. Over."

After they signed off, Greg was not too pleased. "We could be up there with our gear shot out and anchored in Port Burwell if we didn't have to wait for them," he complained.

"That might be true, but we're in this together and together we'll stay. Northern Labrador can be a rough place in the best of times. No place to be alone for sure. We'll soon be passing over a long-liner like this one that's been on the bottom for only three months. She capsized and sank in minutes. The crew would all be lost if it weren't for the company of another boat that plucked them from the water. They saved nothing but the wet clothes on their backs. You don't drive away company in the Labrador Sea, my son," Ben stated, shifting back to the chair.

Greg didn't reply. Instead, he smacked off the lights and quickly disappeared below. I drifted off to sleep.

The lights of the bridge flared on. Coming awake I became aware of the feeling of pins and needles down my deadened left arm. Rolling over onto my back, I rubbed some circulation back into my arm as I watched Don and Ben plot our position on the chart as was the routine at the change of each one-hour watch.

"Steady as she goes on 000 degrees," Ben said, taking a last glance at the radar prior to going below.

"Steady as she goes on 000," Don repeated from his roost in the captain's chair. After settling in, he asked, "Are you asleep, Mick?"

"No," I replied.

"No, and you're not going to get a lot of sleep there, either," he said matter-of-factly, spinning the roost around to face me.

Pushing back the bag, I sat up, rubbed some life back in my arm and replied, "I know. I can feel it in my bones already."

"The last fellow that bunked on that bench was a fisheries observer," Don went on. "We had a lot of wind and high seas that trip and boy, I can tell you, he never got much sleep. His eyes were like two piss holes in a snowbank. After the second day, he took his bedding down and spread it out under the galley table. There wasn't much comfort to be found there. He made a pact with Hector and for the last few days, he'd crawl in Hector's berth and sleep during the times it took to haul back, pick and set the nets."

"What about his duties?" I asked.

Don spun back to check the radar screen. "Duties!" he echoed. "I didn't know he had any," he replied with a smirk on his face. "I heard that you worked for the observer program for a while. You should know more about the observers than I do."

"Yes, but I don't want to go there. I get depressed."

"As bad as that, eh?" Don replied, looking directly at me. "By the way, your watch starts at three o'clock, after Hector."

I wasn't sleepy. Once, I drifted off and came awake to pins and needles and the beckoning beauty of the blazing moon. Pushing off the bag, I sat up and gazed out the windows over my head that overlooked the aft deck. It was a playground for softly shifting shades and shadows. It seemed that the moon had never appeared brighter, nor the sea more tranquil.

Somewhere from afar, a voice said, "Nice night, eh?"

It took a few seconds for my mind to register the words and to respond to Wayne's comment and say, "Times along like these are one of the aspects I love most about being at sea."

"That's right, boy. Later on, when we get farther up north, we'll see the Northern Lights. They're something else, they are."

The trance was broken. Taking a last glance, I slipped back inside my sleeping bag and closed my eyes. The moon let me sleep.

Thursday, August 27

HECTOR DIDN'T HAVE TO CALL ME FOR MY WATCH at 3 a.m. I was washed, a little piss-eyed but wide awake when we plotted our coordinates on the chart. Taking up position in the commander's chair, I observed that the radar was set on the sixteen-mile range. A target was bleeping twelve miles astern. But other than a few shifting specks of sea-clutter, the screen indicated that we were steering a clear course.

"That's the *Vantage* you see there," Hector informed me, pointing at the bleep on the radar screen. "Keep a sharp eye out for growlers. They're the worst, they are. Other than that, steady as she goes."

"Steady as she goes," I repeated as he vacated the cockpit area. "You know how to operate Otto, the autopilot, if you want to alter course in a hurry, don't you? You know, evasive action?"

"Just to be sure, Hector, could you show me?"

"It's simple. Press the button marked 'Manual,' then spin the wheel hard over whichever way you want to go," he said, going through the motions for me.

"I'll do that, Hector, if, God forbid, the occasion arises. Thanks for the demonstration."

"You're welcome. Have a good watch."

"Good night. See you around somewhere tomorrow, maybe."

"Rest assured, we will see each other in the morning cause there's seven fleets of nets to get in fishing order," he said with a grin.

Switching off the lights, he disappeared down the stairway, leaving me alone, on watch, on the bridge of a sixty-five-foot long-liner, nudging apart the lazy ocean swells at 5.2 knots with seven souls sleeping soundly, twenty-seven nautical miles off the Great Northern Peninsula.

The first thing I did was to give the choir a well-deserved

break. This may have been my first watch on the bridge of the *Styx,* but it wasn't my first ship watch ever. The watches on board this boat were short, only an hour long. I reflected back on the four-hours-on, four-hours-off standing watches on ships with my father, Leo. And stand them I did, too, behind the massive ships' wheels trying to manually keep to a relatively straight course. When a ship's bow plunged into the great sea and dived into the trough, the rudder would come clear out of the water. Naturally, gravity made it fall hard-over, causing the wheel to spin viciously like a roulette wheel. This usually resulted in me being hurled clear across the bridge. Then, four short hours off before doing it all over again. Compared to that, this was a piece of cake: sitting back in the commander's comfortable chair, with dual padded armrests, with my feet up on the console, glancing at the radar and the instrument panel, scrutinizing the searchlight beam, letting Otto do his thing.

I stood my first watch at the age of seven. While cruising out of the bay one hot summer day aboard my father's passenger boat, the *Colin II,* Dad overturned a wooden crate on the floor in front of the steering wheel. From this vantage point I could see over the steering wheel and through the window over the bow. He showed me how to steer.

"Steer for that high hill," he'd say before going below or outside on deck, leaving me alone at the helm. As time passed the hill would get closer and closer and just when I was getting afraid, my father would come into the wheelhouse and tell me to alter course and steer towards another hill. In no time it was hill after hill, wave over wave, sea over bow.

Out of the darkness like a ghost in the night, a seabird glided through the searchbeam that lit our course. I kept a lookout for the deadly growler.

Growlers are pieces of icebergs that come in different shapes and sizes. They mean the certain destruction of a ship in a very short time. What makes a growler haunt the dreams of seafarers is the fact that because of its density, it is as hard as granite. Growlers are barely buoyant and float low in the water, making them undetectable by radar. If a ship strikes a growler, the hull is smashed like an eggshell.

My watch passed quickly without growlers, alarm bells, maydays or flashing lights. Time came to call Todd.

The crew's room was stuffy, warm and quiet. Jack snored contentedly from the top bunk on the port; Greg slept comfortably in the bunk underneath. Across the small room, Hector lay snoozing in the lower bunk and Todd was dead to the world in the bunk above him. Grabbing Todd's naked arm, I quietly called him awake. "Todd. Todd. Your watch."

Squinting at me with one eye and rubbing the other eye with the back of his hand, he groggily replied, "Okay."

As I waited on the bridge to be relieved, I checked the searchlight beam. During my watch, three bergs had crept onto the radar screen, two up ahead on the starboard, another, a monster, a titan of the tides, one mile off the port. The blip of the *Vantage* had also snailed up closer to our stern.

Todd came up with a tin of drink and a box of chocolate chip cookies. Placing the lunch on the console, we plotted our position—North 53-27-140 degrees, West 54-27-207 degrees. He pencil pointed to a spot twenty-seven nautical miles north-northeast of us and thirty-five nautical miles from the Grey Islands. Looking at the tiny speck on the chart a feeling of insignificance welled up inside me. We didn't amount to much out here.

"Steady as she goes on 000," I said, moving to my sleeping quarters.

"Steady as she goes on 000," Todd repeated, shifting into the chair with the cookie box nestled in his lap.

Switching off the light I peeled off my clothes and crawled in the sleeping bag.

Sometime later I felt the engine accelerate. The dramatic change in the growl of the Cat diesel and the increased frequency of the vibrations of the hull passing through me seemed to say, "Come on! Enough dragging our ass! There are miles to steam, there's fish to catch. There's money to be had. Come on! Full speed ahead!"

At 7 a.m. I threw back the bag, sat up and rubbed some feeling back into my deadened arm and shoulder. Over the radio a singer sang the words, "… for tonight I sleep on a bed of nails." "How appropriate" was my first thought. It was still beautiful outside. The *Vantage* was within two miles of us cresting the swells with stabilizer arms extended. Offshore seabirds called noddies soared along by us and closely watched the wake. Noddies, also known as Atlantic fulmars, are oceanic birds similar to the gull. About twenty inches long, this beautiful seabird is smoky gray with dark wing tips, and has pale green legs and feet and a yellow bill. The noddy is a transatlantic migrant and can weather the worst of storms on the wing or atop the tossing sea. In flight noddies appear stubby and flap their wings a great deal between short gliding spells. They nest in the cliffs close to shore, where the female lays a single egg. Being scavengers, they have a tendency to trail fishing boats and often feed in a frenzy close beside the hull when crews are pulling gear.

My nose detected frying bacon and my stomach growled. On my way through the galley, Jack, who was standing beside the propane stove, asked, "Will that be two eggs or three?"

"Two will do, thank you," I answered, glad to see that the head was free. Don and Hector were sitting at the table eating their meal when I closed the door behind me.

"Haggard" was a word that popped to mind when I saw my reflection in the mirror. Pushing back my hair, I waited for the sink to fill about three-quarters full with hot water. The face-cloth, towel and toothpaste brought me around. My hairbrush improved my appearance a little.

Ready to face the music, I entered the galley and slipped in behind the table. Hector was accompanying the singers on the television set when Jack placed a ten-dollar breakfast on the table in front of me. "Thank you very much, sir," I said graciously.

"You're welcome, and eat all that now. Get every bit inside your ribs. My son, if you was a turbot and I caught you in a net, I'd throw you back because you'd be too poor to keep."

"Aye, aye, captain," I replied with a grin. Blessing myself, I promptly proceeded to follow orders.

Hector looked at me and said point-blank, "I loves to sing."

Don was picking his teeth. Turning from the screen to face me, he said with a grin, a nod and a wink, "You call that singing? It sounds to me like you're in pain or something. What do you think, Mick? Does he sound like he's in harmony or in agony?"

"You're just jealous that I can sing and you can't," Hector responded, tightening the lid of the jam jar real tight and plac-ing it in the rack.

"Eh, Mick? What do you think?" Don persisted.

"Well, Hector, I'll put it to you this way," I said with a grin. "I say you can sing the best kind and don't ever give up on my account. But take my advice and don't give up your day job."

Finishing the last sip of pop, he tossed the tin out the port-hole and replied, "You likes to sing too, don't ya?"

"Yes, sir. I do like to sing. Music is the universal language."

"Well, you can sing us a song while we're in the hold pulling back nets," Don interjected, shifting from the table with mug and spoon. "No doubt, there will be time for you to sing three or four songs. Did you ever tie together a fleet of gear before?"

"I can remember doing something like that with my father but only on a small scale, and that was a long time ago," I replied. "To say that I'm a little rusty would be an understatement."

"You'll get plenty of practice today, then," Hector stated. "And tomorrow and the next day. There are seven fleets to ready before we get to the fishing grounds. Each fleet has fifty ten-inch mesh nets and each net is fifty fathoms long and three fathoms deep. Add fourteen moorings, each one about a mile long, and I'll say you'll get lots of practice," he said.

The engine room was hot and noisy with the Cat doing all the talking. Slipping off my deck shoes I dressed for the hold.

Hector had the hatch covers off and was singing and shifting things around down below. The crew's suits of rubber clothes swung lazily from steel pegs welded to the superstructure. My suit was hanging from a hook a little distant from the other suits, on the only peg that wasn't in use. I selected the pants and pulled them on. Leaving the coat on the peg, I made my way over to the hold and backed down the aluminum ladder.

The hold was spacious. All the space was divided into sections called pounds. Three pounds up along the port side, three up the center and three along the starboard. Standing in the center pound, I allowed my eyes to adjust to the dim lighting. Jack and Don joined us and the job of tying together a fleet of gear began.

First we organized the place. There was a lot of gear down there. A pound contained metal pound boards about three feet long and eight inches wide, marked to designate which board made each pound. The three aft pounds were chock-full of braided nylon bags each containing one gill net. Two pounds were filled with 5/8-inch nylon rope. Another pound contained a pile of aluminum piping that, when assembled, directed the fish from above into any pound in the hold.

Hector dug out a blue plastic barrel and placed it in the center pound. The barrel was mounted on a set of swivel legs in such a way that it could be easily spun in both directions. The ship's transit through the gentle swells was barely discernible. The vibration of the props rattled the metal pound boards, reminding me of chattering teeth.

"Grab one of those nets, Mick, and empty it out in the barrel. We'll show you how to put a fleet of gear in fishing order," Hector said.

I grabbed one of the bags and stood it up on its end, untied the knot and dumped it in the barrel. Folding up the empty bag, I placed it to one side. The barrel could hardly contain all the monofilament webbing. To keep it from spilling, Hector placed his hands across the top.

Don grabbed the nylon headrope and Jack the nylon footrope. They tied the ends to a stanchion so that they could find them later when it came time to tie on the mooring ropes. Having done so, they both retreated to an empty forward pound that would hold this fleet of gear. In unison, they started to pull back and the net spewed from the barrel.

Don and Jack spread the net evenly and carefully about their feet in such a way as to ensure that the nets did not entangle as they were being shot, or set. Hector spun the barrel this way and that, and most of the twists and snarls of tangled webbing disappeared. A tight tangle in the webbing would require the use of hands. In no time at all, I was reaching for net number two.

After the net was dumped in the barrel and Don and Jack had selected their respective ends, Don asked me, "Do you know how to tie a knot called the Fisherman's bend?"

Shaking my head, I replied, "No."

"Watch how it's done," he said, holding up the two ends. With a few quick deft movements the two fifty-fathom nets were joined into one.

By the time a dozen nets had been pulled back, I, too, was tying Fisherman's bends.

Jack pointed out an end to a huge mound of mooring rope. "Mick, after you tosses those nets in the pound beside Hector, take the end of that mooring rope and tie it to that post so we know where to find it later. Then pull the rope back and coil it up in the side pound, will ya?"

I gladly worked to dig the heavy nets out from their hiding places. Quite often the rotten bags ripped apart when I plucked on them. I started to sweat, and soon my inside clothes lost ground in absorbing the moisture that flowed down my face and back.

"Take your time and hurry up," Hector said, grinning at me. "Nah, take yer time. There's no rush. We got five long days ahead of us. We can do three fleets a day if we had to."

Taking a short spell I noticed that even though the three of them worked methodically and constantly, there wasn't a single bead of sweat on them.

After brief instructions, I began pulling back the mooring rope. The correct procedure was to coil the rope like a lariat. When my hand held five loops, I placed them carefully down at my feet. The next loops were placed beside it and the next beside that one to ensure that the rope did not tangle up when it was shot out. By the time I had one hundred fathoms spread evenly about the pound floor, I was exhausted.

As we assembled the fleet the crew talked amongst themselves. I did my work and listened. When conversation stopped and only the metal pound boards chattered, Hector would sing.

"My God, Hector! I hope you don't make Him mad singing His glory as bad as that," Don said, with humor in his voice.

"Yer just jealous cause you can't sing," Hector countered.

"No way can anyone be jealous of a noise like that," Don teased. "Mick, you can do better than that. Come on, now's your chance."

At first I was a little reluctant to take the floor, but it seemed they wanted me in. "Okay, I'll sing you a song, bearing in mind that I do not even hope to hold a candle to Hector." Then, cheerily, I took my rhythm from the sea, resumed pulling back the mooring rope and started to sing lightheartedly an old ballad about the sea.

They stopped to listen for a while. By the time I reached the chorus a second time, everyone had resumed work and was singing along. Things were looking good. Possibly in seven or eight short weeks I'd be home again, more independent and proud as a peacock. If all went well, then maybe they'd take me more often. Who knew? Maybe this time next year, my income would be in the eighty-thousand-dollar bracket. The thought inspired and uplifted me and I finished the folk song in crescendo.

"You're a good singer," Hector said, "but don't give up your day job."

"I hear what you're saying."

We sang at least a dozen songs, and Hector never faltered on a verse. About then, I found the end of the mile-long mooring rope.

"Tie those ends onto the stanchion so we know where they are. Then, take that end there and tie it on there and do the same thing again," Don said, pulling back in perfect sync with Jack. "Thirteen more moorings and over three hundred nets to go."

∿∿∿∿∿∿∿∿∿∿∿∿∿∿∿∿

After dinner, I sat on the rope coiled in a crab pot on the spot behind the bridge that had a panoramic view of the ocean. The *Vantage* had crept to within a mile of our stern and maintained a steady course a few points off to starboard. A flurry of seabirds wheeled and whirled all around the ship, intently watching the foaming wake for any edible scraps.

Conditions were serene and peaceful on the eastern fringes of the North Atlantic Ocean through Iceberg Alley. I felt that it couldn't be much better sailing on a Caribbean cruise. In my line of sight I counted ten icebergs of different shapes and sizes. The closest, but far from the stateliest, was passing less than a mile to port. Like a gleaming, jagged tooth it stuck up to a height of a hundred feet or more.

Close beside the ship, movement caught my attention. Two seabirds, murres, a mother and its chick, were fleeing from the encroachment of the ship. Looking about, I saw that the sea was alive with them.

Snick! Snick! Snick! Snick! It sounded like small arms fire coming from the bow. A pang of apprehension surfaced. I walked forward apprehensively to see Greg shooting at the murres with a .22-caliber automatic rifle. Spent brass casings tinkled on the steel deck. Bullet bubbles formed close to the fleeing birds.

"You're shooting behind her!" Ben shouted from inside the bridge.

Taking the rifle from his shoulder, Greg turned towards Ben and replied sarcastically, "I can see that, Dad! They're hard to hit."

Surprised and shocked, I walked right up beside him and asked, "What are you doing, Greg?"

"What does it look like? I'm having a few shots," he replied curtly, looking directly at me.

Suddenly, my brain registered the full impact of his reply. The message came loud and clear: "This is our boat! We'll do as we like and you got nothing to say about it!"

Speechless, I retreated aft and watched the shoot out of the line of fire.

The sound of gunfire drew Todd to the foredeck armed with a twelve-gauge semiautomatic shotgun. Before long, the breeze carried the harmonies of the gospel choir mixed with gunfire and the ocean was transformed into a slaughterhouse for families of unsuspecting murres.

Suddenly, this was no longer a nice day. Suddenly, this was not such a nice crew. This was not a nice ship. This was not going to be a good trip.

Boom. Boom. Boom. Snick. Snick. Snick.

Through the cloud of gloom and doom that suddenly shrouded me, Hector shouted, "Mick, come down in the hold!"

Hector was alone when I fumed down the ladder and stood beside him in the center pound. I couldn't keep what I had just witnessed inside me. "Hector, I see the boys don't mind shooting the birds," I said in a tone of voice that didn't disguise my disappointment and growing resentment.

Hector was a big, burly man—barrel-chested, strong and agile. With venom, he snatched a net bag from the floor and threw it in the barrel. The upward pull to empty out the net tore the bottom out of the braided bag. "You noticed that, eh?" he said, as he tossed the shredded bag in the pile with the other rejects.

"You'd have to be deaf, dumb, blind, stupid and maggoty drunk not to notice," I blurted. "Jesus Christ, what kind of crowd are they to shoot birds for target practice? I thought clay pigeons were used for that."

"Not this crowd," Hector replied. "They shoot at everything, and I mean everything, that comes in range of the rails. It's shocking. You'll see for yourself. I don't like it. I don't take any part in it," he said in what seemed to be a frustrated tone of voice.

"Well, well, well, wouldn't you know? That's just my luck. I thought this was a good ship. Jesus Christ," I swore.

Hector caught my eye and said, "I understand how you feel, but let me tell you something. The squeaky wheel don't get the grease onboard this one. It gets replaced, and if you got anything to say about what you see or what goes on at sea aboard this ship, I'd advise you to say nothing until you're back on dry land."

"Thanks for the advice, Hector," I replied, realizing the truth of what he said. "What I'd like to know from you, Hector, is, being a religious man, how can you keep from telling?"

His big hands stayed on the barrel of linnet. "Do you drink, Mick?" he asked.

"What's that have to do with it? From what I understand drinking aboard this ship is a sure way to get put ashore permanently, so you can't tell me that alcohol is to blame for the death of those birds."

"Do ya go to church?" he asked sullenly.

"Yes, Hector, I do."

"I used to be a hard case," he confessed. "There was nothing I wouldn't drink or smoke! And drugs! I've handled, smoked, baked, shot, sold and ate more than you weigh. And fight! I'd sooner fight than eat. One Saturday, me and my buddies was on a tear that lasted all night. I tried to make it home but collapsed in a ditch beside the road. Not knowing anything, I felt someone trying to wake me. Coming to what little sense I had, I realized it was the pastor. With his hand on my shoulder, he bent down and looked into my face. 'Drunk again, eh, Hector?' he said.

"I looked as straight as I could into his eyes and replied, 'Yes, Pastor, me, too.'"

I burst out laughing. I couldn't help it. "You never, Hector! What did he say?"

With not the least hint of a smile, he replied, "He told me 'Get up out of the gutter! Look at yourself. What would your mother think?'"

Listening and trying desperately hard not to laugh, I ventured, "So you straightened up and followed him to church."

"No. I told him to get his hands off me!"

I burst out laughing again. Hector never cracked a smile. The ladder shook and rattled. Todd and Greg backed down and stood beside us in the pound. All humor deserted me.

"What are you laughing at, boys?" Todd asked. Greg didn't say anything. He grabbed the footrope and began to tie it to the fleet.

"I wasn't laughing," Hector replied. "Mick asked me a question and I was giving him an answer which, evidently, he thought was kind of funny."

"I'm sorry if I offended you, Hector, but, I think what you said is funny, although I know it's no laughing matter. Maybe we'll talk later."

"That's fine with me," he said.

With ropes in hand, Todd and Greg retreated to the pound. The webbing spewed from the spinning barrel and the hold was again full of the sounds of men working gear. Hector began to sing.

~~~~~~

Greg and Todd didn't like each other all that much. Unlike Don and Jack, they hardly spoke to one another while they pulled back the nets. Todd was in the mood for chitchat. Greg seemed glum. Maybe it was because he had finished second in the shoot.

"Did you get a moose license this year?" Todd asked me in a voice that sounded as friendly and genuine as could be.

I wasn't eager to chat to him, but we were sailing in a small boat upon an immense and unforgiving ocean with a long trip ahead. As congenial as I could be, I replied, "Yes, I did." The braided nylon bag tore in my hands.

"What area?" he continued.

"Behind my house."

"Area Twenty-Two, is it?"
~~~~~~

"Yes."

"Lots of moose in there?" he inquired.

"No, boy, not lots," I heard myself say, "but we manage to fill our tags when we're lucky enough to get them."

"I'm living down the road from you now and we're looking to buy a house. Any good houses for sale around where you lives?"

I thought to say, "If there was a thousand for sale, I wouldn't tell you. All I need now is the likes of you living within gunshot of me." Instead, I said, "No, boy, not that I know of, although there are plenty of homes for sale around town. You shouldn't have any trouble finding one to buy."

"We'll have to get together and go hunting sometime," he suggested.

Greg seemed intent on nothing other than getting the work done. Todd fell behind and Greg stopped pulling back. Todd caught up; the work continued.

"I wouldn't take him huntin' with ya if I was you," Greg interjected.

"I wouldn't want to go with *you*," Todd shot back.

"I wouldn't ask you to go with me," Greg countered.

To efficiently pull back a net, both the head and footropes must be pulled back in unison. If one person slows, stops or falls behind, the other rope will slacken quickly and fall to the floor. Greg seemed to vent his frustrations by increasing the speed of his hand-over-hand motions. Todd fell behind again. The flow stopped.

"And never mind yer back talk! Use your hands instead of your tongue and do something useful," Greg snarled, as he waited for Todd to catch up.

Even in the dinginess of a fish pound while busy at work, I recognized the symptoms of the dreaded curse of seasickness. All mariners react differently to the constant motion of the sea. The curse overcomes some as soon as they encounter the first ocean swells. Some stomachs are turned by the transit of the ship; others by the smells of food, diesel fumes and high levels of heat. Some mariners weather the curse quickly and are never bothered by it again. Some never get used to it and are plagued constantly.

It seemed to me that Todd had developed all the symptoms rather quickly. His face turned crimson. Sweat beads popped out on his glistening forehead. The flow of the webbing stopped and Todd got sick and sprayed the nets with vomit. Greg hopped out of the pound checking to see if any had gotten on him.

Todd was gasping for breath. "Oh, God, I'm some sick," he groaned.

"Get up on deck!" Hector bawled. "We got to work down here!"

"Yes, get up, wimp!" Greg added like salt to a wound. "Don't be throwing up yer stinkin' guts down here! Get up out of it!"

Todd stumbled out of the pound with his eyes running brooks of water and his face white. Groping for the ladder he escaped up into the daylight two rungs at a time. I had to laugh.

"He's gone for the day, now," Greg said in a voice that made no attempt to disguise his disgust.

"Mick, you pull back with Greg. I'll handle the nets," Hector suggested.

Climbing in the pound, Greg asked, "Are you left-handed or right-handed?"

"What difference does it make?" I replied.

"A lot."

"Right," I answered.

"Well, you take the footrope and stand over here," he said, throwing the rope down and crossing over to stand next to me.

Moving to the other side of the pound, I picked up the footrope and the flow started. Almost immediately I fell behind. Try as I might, the rope fell slack before my bare hand could reach it. Each time Greg stopped and waited for me to catch up. By the time the end flicked out of the barrel, I was sweating bullets. While they tied the knots, I took off a layer of clothes.

Greg began to pull ahead again and my frustration and pent-up emotions soared. Intentionally, Greg stopped. "You sure you're right-handed?" he asked. "You try on this side. You might really be left-handed," he said, laughing.

Moving to change places with him, my boots snarled in a mesh. Down I fell atop Todd's vomit. Jumping to my feet as if I had landed on a red-hot stove, I snarled out a litany of blasphemy that even startled me. The laughter died abruptly. "If my father hears you cursing like that, you'll be put ashore," he said.

Put ashore! The words echoed in my head. After killing a dozen murres for the hell of it, you tell me that I'll be put ashore if I swears! Well, that's one way to end this nightmare right now! I was primed and ready with as many verses of curses that I was sure would get me ashore at light speed. They were at the very tip of my tongue when Hector started to sing and I was reminded of his advice.

Some sense came back to me and I heard myself say, "I apologize for that. That's what I get for laughing at Todd: his regurgitated dinner all over my clothes."

No one replied. Taking the rungs of the ladder two at a time, I went up into the daylight to wash down with the hose. A covey of noddies flew about Todd's hunched form.

<hr>

As I was battling to keep from falling behind in the hold, Newfoundland was falling behind in the wake. Off to port was the barren, rugged southern coast of the Big Land, Labrador.

At supper, a hockey game blared on the television set as I squeezed in next to Hector. Wayne, it seemed, loved hockey as much as he loved hymns and had brought several tapes of the Canada-Russia series. It was a tie game with no goals scored.

His eyes were glued to the set. A Russian checked a Canadian player to the ice. In retaliation, a Canadian comrade bashed the Russian against the boards, buckling the Plexiglas. A fight ensued. Wayne roared, "Kill it! Yes, kill it! Leave 'em alone ref!" Everyone stopped eating to watch the beating.

After order was restored and penalties were assessed, Wayne, with knife in hand, reached across the table for the loaf of bread and asked, "Do you watch hockey, Mick?"

"No, not as a follower like that," I replied. "I used to be a fan of the Leafs until the teams became too plentiful to keep track of, and when it was more sport, less business. To tell you the truth, Wayne, the only time I can sit down and watch a game is when I know the Stanley Cup is in the building. I see you like it."

"Yes, I loves it, loves it. The rougher the better," he said.

Canada scored and Wayne clapped his hands in delight. "Hooray!" he chortled. "Take that now, ye bunch of dirt bags! Put that in your pipe and smoke it!" Everyone was happy to see Canada score. No one mentioned the seabirds that were shot and killed just a few hours ago. I slipped out during the first intermission, opting to finish my tea alone, topside.

The sun was mere inches above the blue hills of Labrador. I counted fourteen icebergs in sight. The summit of one gigantic berg was as flat as a tabletop, and soared into the sky. Even from five miles away, its glow was ominous. A small plane could have landed on its flat top.

The *Vantage* was keeping pace with us. Painted blue and white like the *Styx*, she blended in perfectly with the seascape. With the stabilizer arms suspended, she took on the look of a small bird attempting to take flight. Black smoke from the stack smudged the azure sky. I saw no murres. Noddies scouted for scraps in the wake. There was a chill in the air. It was beginning to feel like fall.

Plop! Plop! Two bags of garbage splashed in the foam below me and fell away astern. I had just lit a cigarette when Jack came out of the wheelhouse and closed the door behind him.

"You having a smoke, Mick?"

"Yep, want one?"

"No, but I'll have a draw."

"I didn't know you smoked," I said somewhat surprised. As far as I was aware, being religious men, there were no smokers or drinkers aboard, except for me. Smoking was permitted only outside on deck.

"No one else aboard does, either," he replied. When I made the motion to pass the cigarette, he declined taking it. "Not here. Let's go over there by the rail."

In the shelter of the bridge we shared a cigarette.

"Thanks for that," he said, tossing the butt over the rail and heading back inside.

"Anytime," I said.

My bedroom seemed to be the site of some kind of jam session. Through the bridge windows, I could see Ben slumped in the commander's chair. Greg was standing beside him. Don sat on my bench playing a guitar. With my empty mug in hand, I climbed down the ladder through the open hatch to the sheltered deck and entered the galley to wash my mug. From there I went to the washroom to wash my other mug and brush my teeth. Then I joined them in my room as Don struck a loud chord and boisterously sang the opening verse of "Dropkick Me Jesus through the Goalposts of Life." Ben seemed to enjoy it.

Just then, the radio blared, "All stations. All stations. All stations. This is the marine weather forecast issued by Environment Canada. For Belle Isle, light westerly winds, ten to fifteen knots, shifting to northwesterly, winds twenty-five knots early Friday morning. Temperature low: tonight, 4°C, high for Friday, 10°C."

"Very good day on the way. With a week of good weather, we'd be up to Port Burwell alongside the *Bakur*, waiting for our nets to fill," Ben said in a voice drenched with optimism.

"We'd be up there with a load of fish if we never had to slow in and wait for the *Vantage*," Greg grumbled.

"Greg, don't be talking like that!" Ben countered. "We're in this together and together we'll stay. The little time lost waiting for the *Vantage* is neither here nor there, my son."

"What's the *Bakur*?" I asked

"That's the collector boat that's moored at Port Burwell waiting to take our turbot as soon as we can bring them in," Don answered, striking a softer chord as the sun went out in a blaze of glory.

~~~~~~

At 9 p.m. we were abeam of and twenty-two nautical miles off Frenchman's Island, maintaining a sure course at a speed of 8.3 knots on a quiet sea. Before following Greg below, Don said to me, "The watches are posted there on the console. You comes on at 3 a.m., after Hector."

Friday, August 28

I COULDN'T SLEEP. I spent most of Hector's watch peering out the window from the rumble seat. With fifteen growlers on the screen four eyes are always better than two.

Coughing abruptly as if to clear his throat, Hector turned towards me and said, "Mick, I've been thinkin' about what you said today about not squealin' on the boys."
~~~~~~

"So have I. What's on your mind?"

"You have children, don't you?" he asked.

"Yes, I do," I replied. "Two teenagers. You have a couple your-self, don't you?"

"Yes. My daughter, Karen, is sixteen and my little fellow, Justin, is two. I misses him already," he said rubbing his heart. "Instead of paying my taxes last year, I renovated my house. Now, I'm behind a lot of money. If I tells, I'm gone and it's all gone."

Turning only my head to face him, I said, "I know what you're saying, Hector. I had the same problem years ago when I was a warden on the river. I'm sure you heard about it. I paid a heavy price for speaking out. But it's my feeling that we're obli-gated to look out the creatures, Hector. Christ, you want to be able to show Justin a whale, or a murre, don't ya?"

He never replied. His mind and gaze seemed to be out some-where before the bow. I persisted. "Don't ya, Hector?"

"Yes! Of course I do!" he blurted, shifting uncomfortably in the chair.

"Well, it's fellows like us who witness the wasteful destruc-tion that must at least try to stop it."

"Well, like I told you before, if I was you, I wouldn't squeak too loud until this trip is over," he said, turning to look directly into my eyes.

"I hear you, Hector, but squeak I will."

~~~~~~

The ocean was as still as a millpond when I dressed at 7 a.m. The morning sky held promise of a good day on the way. It was as nice as it could possibly get in the Labrador Sea. But I didn't get to see much of it for after breakfast, it was back to the hold with Hector, Jack and Don.

While working away, Don said, "This is as far north as I've ever been. How about you, Mick?"
~~~~~~

"I've been further north once, when I sailed with my father on the *Clyde* to Iqaluit, Frobisher Bay, with the settlement's yearly supply of beer and liquor and fifty new snowmobiles."

"Everyone there must have been eager to help unload," Hector said.

The end flicked from the barrel and I emptied another net in. The rotten bag ripped, so I threw it in the pile with the other forty rejects.

"They sure were. The tides up in Frobisher Bay drop thirty feet. The *Clyde* was constructed with a flat bottom. The day before our arrival a bulldozer cleared a spot in the harbor of boulders and large rocks. At high tide we anchored at that spot in the harbor. When the tide fell the ship was sitting high and dry with the ocean about a mile away. While the tide was out, trucks came right up alongside and we discharged the cargo directly into them."

"I don't disbelieve it for a minute," Jack said. "How's the tides going to treat our fishing gear, I wonder? How many of these nets will never be seen again?"

Trying not to sound too pessimistic I replied, "I don't know about that, but my impression is that it's not an easy environment to eke out a living from."

"I guess it's like Ben said, we'll know more in a month or two," Don said.

About half a fleet later, a building sea caused the hull to lunge and plunge. Vibrations shivered back from the bow. Not having found my sea legs, I had to battle for stability. Sailors have a saying: in fair seas it's one hand for me and one hand for the ship; in mad seas, it's two hands for me, fook the ship. For me, most of the time, it was one hand for me and one hand for the ship.

~~~~~~
~~~~~~

By four o'clock, three fleets were in fishing order, putting us well ahead of schedule. It was becoming a little too uncomfortable in the hold, so we decided to quit for the evening. Don came up from the hold carrying sixty torn and shredded net bags. Without delay he swaggered to the rail and threw them over the side where the whitecaps chewed into them.

As I watched them a pang of guilt surfaced. Everyone knows that nylon and plastic are the scourges of the sea. Such materials seem to last forever. Countless numbers of sea creatures come afoul of this garbage and die as a direct result. Some creatures become entangled, suffocate and drown. Others confuse the garbage as food and swallow it and suffer a long, painful death. Everybody knew that but, still and all, there were sixty nylon bags set free to haunt the high seas for the near eternity.

"Tikaoralik" in Inuit means big river, and on the chart it shows a sheltered bay of good anchorage. Into its deepest recess we glided just before dark to escape the forecasted wind. Fifty-knot northerlies would not have stopped the *Styx*, but it would be rough enough for the *Vantage*. Ben chose to seek shelter here.

Astern in Iceberg Alley, a flotilla of forty-two icebergs studded the sea. Never before had I seen so many. Some loomed up like gargantuan cathedrals with spires spiking the stormy skies. Others were specks, barely discernible in the wild gray expanse of it all.

In the lee of a naked island, about a mile from shore, Ben stopped the ship. On signal, Wayne and Hector released the brakes on both port and starboard winches and the iron doors strapped to the stern that doubled as anchors dropped to the seabed. The otter boards, as they're known, each weigh about a ton and are towed behind the ship when dragging. They are designed to keep the mouth of the net open as they are dragged over the seafloor. Before the *Styx* had tightened on her cables, up until darkness fell, Greg and Todd were out on the bow with their guns, eager to try their marksmanship on anything that happened to fly by. The *Vantage* anchored about a mile away.

Excited and expectant conversations on the bridge that evening revolved mostly around the wildlife that could possibly be in there for the taking. The plan for tomorrow was to go ashore in the speedboat and have a hunt around. The chart depicted a pond close to the beach. Todd and Greg planned to take their fishing rods to try to catch a fry of trout.

The last man went below for the night at 11 p.m. Outside, at coordinates N 54-55-486, W 58-42-380, overcast skies made for a dark night with not a single star. The temperature was 2°. On gusts of wind it was easy to detect the smell of vegetation. It felt like fall. Tikaoralik was a lonely river. The only lights to be seen were those of the *Vantage*, huddled in the shadows. I wondered who had been here last and why? What was still here? What would we encounter tomorrow on our escapade ashore?

Saturday, August 29

THE BRIDGE WAS CHILLY WHEN I SAT UP and glanced through the windows at seven o'clock. The shroud of fog had lifted or blown away, exposing a land completely devoid of trees. Low shrubbery, adorned in fall foliage, provided a dab of color to the otherwise drab landscape that spread out above the beach to the lowlands in the foreground and on to the distant highlands. Not only could I smell the tundra, I could see it. Except for the exposed granite summits and windblown rocky outcropping, the tundra covered everything. There wasn't a sign of human habitation. We had the land of the Big River all to ourselves.

Todd and I shared cleanup duties after breakfast. As he was going through the door with a garbage bag in his hand, I asked him, "Have you ever heard of recycle and reuse?"

"Yes, but that don't apply out here. Here the motto is, 'No deposit, no return.' It's strictly an open door policy, if you know what I mean," he replied before disappearing outside with the bag.

No one had to tell Todd twice to get the speedboat ready. He and Greg had the fifteen-horsepower outboard fueled and ready for launching in jig time. Then, using the boom, they hoisted up the fourteen-foot aluminum craft and lowered it over the lee side.

"Want to go ashore, Mick?" Ben asked.

For a change of scenery, I replied, "Sure, I'll go."

The bay was choppy and sea spray soaked us before we made our way in the overloaded speedboat to a rocky beach where the chart depicted a pond. Greg was first to set foot ashore just before Todd eagerly clambered out.

We pulled in the speedboat and waited until Todd returned from the pond to report somewhat disappointedly, "No geese, ducks or caribou." The cove was rimmed with low shrubs that reminded me of bonsai boreal spruce groomed and manicured by Mother Nature. The last of the great boreal forest was not all that impressive. Standing about waist high, the vegetation seemed as if it was cuddled together for protection. It was almost impossible to force a way through.

The easiest route to the pond was up a small brook that flowed out and pooled before breaching the beach and flowing into the sea. Along both banks grew a stunted form of alder that glowed golden in its autumn splendor.

Once through the thicket the wide open spaces of the arctic tundra stretched for miles and miles, except in those exposed places where the winds and weather had worn the soil away to expose the bare granite. It was towards one of those bald summits that I headed. Ben followed.

Walking on tundra is quite different from walking on the deck of a ship. Like walking on a mattress, my boots sank in deep. Tundra covers some of the harshest landscapes on the globe, yet this vegetation is very fragile. It shattered beneath my boot before giving way to my weight. When I lifted my boot to make another, step, my bootprint remained. It would take years, if not forever, for the damage to repair.

From the rocky bluff Ben and I had a commanding view of the land that stretched, rose and faded into the mist. In all its vastness there wasn't a tree to be seen. Expanses of fresh water lay everywhere.

Todd and Greg had put aside their guns and were fitting out their fishing rods. Todd's hook splashed the surface of the pond a few seconds before Greg's lure. Both became hooked in the bottom at about the same time and in no time the pond claimed two expensive lures. In unison, they put away the rods, took up their guns and strolled about.

Beside me, Ben stood scanning the landscape intently with binoculars. With what I took to be a great degree of disappointment, he said, "There's not a thing alive to be seen. You'd think you'd see a caribou in a place like this, wouldn't you?"

"Yes," I replied. "This is the home of the George River herd and for the life of me I can't understand how they can exist eating lichen."

Picking a sample from the ground beside me I held it in my hands. It reminded me in some ways of coral. Bone-white in color, brittle, fragile, slow-growing and nearly featherweight. To my eye there wasn't one bit of nourishment or sustenance contained within. Still and all, caribou grow fat and multiply eating it.

"Well, I'd like to see a big stag come prancing by about now," Ben said, cradling the 308 Remington rifle. "There might be caribou behind that other rise," he said, scratching his head and looking in that direction. "I think I'll go take a look."

Snick. Snick. Snick. Clearly to my ears came the familiar sound of small arms fire followed by Todd's booming voice as he shouted at the top of his lungs, "Greg, don't shoot! I'm here Greg, don't shoot!"

By the time I had turned in the direction of the commotion, the rifle fired three more times. About fifty yards away, Greg stood in the thicket and aimed his rifle in Todd's direction, at the tundra on the far side of the pond.

Another two rapid reports brought another yell from Todd wanting Greg to stop firing as he dived for the ground to seek cover.

In reaction, I called, "Greg! What are you doing?"

When he turned in my direction, a scary feeling swept over me. I thought he was going to fire at me and my heart filled with anxiety.

Greg didn't fire. After what seemed an icy eternity, he drew back in the thicket and disappeared.

I was shaken up.

Todd must have been watching from under cover because the branches had no sooner closed behind Greg before he was on his feet hollering, "Greg, my son, I'm telling your father you tried to shoot me. My son, you're not fit to have a gun! Ben! Ben!" he roared. "Take the gun from Greg before he shoots somebody!"

Ben heard Todd hollering and passed me by in full stride. "What's going on?" he demanded in a surly voice.

From another direction Jack called out, "Bakeapples! Look at all the bakeapples. Come over and help me pick them."

Bakeapples, often called cloudberries, are the fruit of the tundra. I ignored Jack and followed Ben through the thicket to the beach where Todd now crouched behind a boulder. When

Ben approached the beach, Todd broke cover and ran towards him, blurting out the story every step of the way.

When Todd had told Ben of the harrowing experience with the glancing bullets, Ben asked me if what Todd was saying was true. My response was that although I could not see how close the glancing bullets were coming to Todd, the rest of the story was true.

"Where's Greg now?" Ben asked.

"I don't know. I haven't seen him since he tried to shoot me," Todd replied.

"I haven't, either," I volunteered looking around somewhat apprehensively.

A hundred yards up the windy beach a large rock stuck up like a headstone. In its lee, with a soft cushion of fragrant vegetation to sit on, we waited and watched.

Jack arrived with close to a gallon of bakeapples in a plastic bag. Todd blurted out the story to him. He seemed not the least bit surprised.

A flock of twenty eider ducks flew past. They are the largest of the North American ducks and are hunted in the fall by hunters using speedboats. In years past, so plentiful were they that it was said, "When they went to wing the day was darkened."

Shortly afterwards, the distinct sound of small arms fire carried on the wind. Todd shouted, "There's Greg up there!"

Ben called out his name. Greg seemed not to hear. Ben waved his arms. Greg seemed not to see. Ben shouted and waved. Greg dragged his ass all the way back.

A big row between Todd and Greg ensued as to who did what to whom. Ben put a forceful stop to it by taking the rifle from Greg, saying, "You can't be at that, my son. You could shoot somebody. You needs to take a hunter safety course or something. I can't have stupid gunplay. If it happens again, you'll never again clamp your finger around a gun in my company. You hear me, Greg?"

Greg heard him, but he didn't like it and stormed away towards the speedboat. It was time to go.

We arrived back aboard the *Styx* soaking wet and empty-handed except for the bakeapples. At the galley table, Todd blurted out to Wayne his version of what happened. Greg shouted his own version, but Wayne sided with Todd. Greg was warned again about gunplay before he stormed off to his room.

That evening, alone on the bridge, I lay on the bench waiting for sleep and reliving the events of the day. I realized that, in the days and weeks to come, I would have to be on guard against not only the dangers of being at sea in the strange world of offshore gillnetting, but also of being shot. The realization didn't warm me. This crew was as Hector had said; "They will shoot anything."

I realize there is a time in most everyone's life when stupid or thoughtless things are done. I have shot my share of birds with BB guns and I have jigged a number of salmon. Up to a certain point in my life, I used to sneak around the woods at night with my gun, light and pocketknife intent upon poaching.

I learned the dirty tricks of the trade from the people I spent time with—my father and my friends. And some of the dirty tricks I thought up on my own accord and taught them to others.

Eventually I realized that it was not right, and I stopped doing it at around the age of seventeen. Now I hunt only for food and, occasionally, for profit, as in sealing and fishing. To witness such wasteful practices and downright cruel behavior towards the birds shocked me. It's the age-old adage in shining colors: "If it moves shoot it, if it don't chop it down." Destroy a ton to ice a pound. I spent time trying to figure it out until words a friend once said echoed inside my head: "Some people learn early. Some learn late. Others never learn."

Sunday, August 30

SHORTLY AFTER MIDNIGHT, MY BREATH appeared like smoke in the glare of the deck lights as I stood out of the way on the shelter deck watching the crew get the *Styx* underway. In a few minutes the otter boards appeared on the surface in a cloud of mud and after a few hand signals and a clanging of iron, both were secured to the hull like a bird tucking in its wings. The winch brakes were dogged down tight. "Doors up!" Wayne shouted. Astern, the black water swirled and foamed as we got underway leaving the Big River behind.

The *Vantage* followed us out to sea to resume our original course, fifty miles out in Iceberg Alley. The wind, still thirty knots strong, whipped up whitecaps that infested the backs of the sixteen-foot swells, causing the *Styx* to kick up her heels a little. The bow plied each and every consecutive wall of water apart at a speed of 8.7 knots. The "fish" that hung from the end of the chain extended from the stabilizers to a depth of five fathoms and ironed out a measure of the ship's pitching. Fish are made of plate iron welded to a round cylinder, weigh about seventy pounds and resemble an airplane. When the fish are out, the ship's speed is slowed by two knots. While they do ease the rolling abeam, they do little to lessen the stem-to-stern plunging and rearing. Foaming green saltwater and spray assaulted all forward windows in the bridge with a crash that drowned out all other noises on an average of seven times a minute. When the bow dove deep and a shudder coursed through the steel hull, just as the sea crashed onto the windows, I and my nylon sleeping bag shifted forward on the bench. As the bow rose, I did not shift back. It was going to be a rough ride. When sleep did come, the forward dipping action almost tossed me out on the floor.

By the time my watch came at 4 a.m., I was glad to get up. Standing with feet shoulder-width apart, I held onto the back of the commander's chair, and watched Otto work. There wasn't much to see in the spotlight through the windows other than black and sour-milk-white. Seven times a minute all front windows foamed with seawater and the bridge was flooded with the sound that hundreds of gallons of water makes when it slams into glass inches from your face. The radar screen was flecked with bergs and sea-clutter, and I scrutinized the erratic search-beam for growlers and berg bits wondering how the hell I was going to see them out there in the turmoil.

By 8 a.m. when I pushed off the sleeping bag to get up to face the day I had figured out why the area through which we plunged on the chart was called the Labrador Marginal Trough. It was because of the "marginal" amount of rest anyone who sleeps on a bench gets while cruising upon it.

After breakfast, I dressed for the hold and the morning was spent with Hector, Jack and Don at the gear.

"Hector, would there happen to be a piece of foam aboard that I might spread out on my bench under my sleeping bag to keep me from slipping forward?" I asked during one of those times when the pound boards were doing most of the talking.

"I don't think so," he replied. "If I remembers correctly, Todd's bunk don't have any foam at all. He lies on a sleeping bag."

"Very good," I replied, disappointed. "Wouldn't you know?"

Don said, "If I was you, I'd bring my bedding down and sleep under the table in the galley."

"No sir," I replied. "That ain't going to happen."

"I hope you brought an extra blanket because it gets awfully cold up there on account of all the windows," Jack put in.

"No, I didn't bring anything else." The end of the net flicked from the barrel.

That evening at 4 p.m. six fleets were in fishing order and only fifty bags remained. The assembled fleets filled two pounds completely and the mooring rope filled another.

From my vantage point on the crab pot, the Labrador headlands appeared almost alongside. The chart showed these heights to soar three thousand feet and we could see them clearly at fifty miles.

The evening was overcast. The wind, although it had diminished some, had an edge to it and made the sea choppy. Twenty icebergs broke the monotony. Two miles astern the *Vantage* kept pace, disappearing in the troughs and rising in a burst of spray. Seagulls accompanied us watching the wake, all appearing not the least bit distressed by the turbulence. What an empty place the sea would be if they were not there.

Off to starboard, amid the mist, whitecaps and spindrifts, my eyes detected a plume of spray shooting into the sky. It was a whale. Of all the beautiful creatures of the sea, I loved to watch whales most of all. The plume dispersed in the wind and I watched to spot it again. A few swells later, the whale blew again and I strained to see it. The spindrift and the distance denied me the pleasure. As empty, hostile and inhospitable as the environment seemed to be up here, it wasn't devoid of life.

Inside the bridge, I watched the darkness close in. I found that the crew respected each other's privacy, as it was so scarce. If you didn't want to talk, that was fine by them. I wasn't in the mood for talking or singing. I tried not to listen.

I spent the time sadly realizing that there would be no place for me here with this crew. There would be no eighty thousand dollars a year and no fancy clothes for Beulah to wear. In reality, I was back to square one, still looking for work, facing out-migration.

In the meantime, I had to work and to look out for myself, watch my bobber and survive to get home again. It wasn't going to be easy, but I had to learn to bite my tongue, say as little as possible, and watch and see exactly what happens at sea onboard an offshore fishing vessel.

I'd watch and record and, in time, tell of today's fishery. I had done it before and nothing was more certain than the fact that I would bite the same dog twice for exactly the same reasons.

With the resolution made, a wave of relief washed over me. The hull dived deep with a starboard plunge and all front windows burst to foam. I shed my clothes and crawled in the sleeping bag. Each time the windows washed, my sleeping bag and I slipped slightly forward.

Monday, August 31

IN THE SHAKE, RATTLE AND ROLL OF THE HOLD, Hector, Jack, Don and I worked until two o'clock getting fleet number seven in fishing order. All was ready. The fleets would be shot straight out of the hold into the sea.

At 6 p.m., abeam of and fifty miles off South Aulatsivic Island, Ben altered course by setting coordinates for the fishing grounds, one hundred and ten nautical miles farther offshore. This change of course brought the seas to the port bow and the plunging gave way to side-to-side rolling that, in spite of the fish, listed us out to thirty-five degrees and sprayed the windows about four times a minute.

That evening from my perch on the crab pot, I watched the land disappear astern. One swell the land was there, the next swell it was gone. A sort of queasy, uneasy feeling welled up inside me as, to no avail, I stood up to catch a final fleeting glimpse. Everywhere was sea. About a mile off the starboard the *Vantage* offered some degree of security.

Dusk caught me lying on my bench. As the searchlight flared on, Ben tuned in the radio to learn the forecast. "All stations. All stations. All stations," a tiny voice came loud and clear over the set. "Marine weather forecast issued by Environment Canada, Goose Bay 10 p.m.... for tonight and Friday...Hamilton Banks ...winds diminishing overnight to westerly ten to fifteen, increasing to twenty-five knots in the evening. Temperature lows, 6°C."

"Good day coming tomorrow," Don stated just before striking a chord on the guitar.

"Yes," Ben replied from the commander's chair. "Good day to shoot the gear. Hopefully the weather will hold civil and we'll get a good fall out of it. Good Lord willing, we'll have the gear fishing and be in Port Burwell to rendezvous with the *Bakur* in a few days."

Keying the mike, he hailed, "*Vantage, Vantage, Vantage. Styx*, read Jerry? Over."

Quietly Don played another soft chord or two. "*Styx*, this is the *Vantage*. Twenty-one-eighty-two, Ben."

"Roger."

The gist of the conversation that followed was lost to slumber.

Tuesday, September 1

DISAPPOINTMENT HAUNTED ALL MY DREAMS. I came awake in a panic. Hector was at the helm.

"I don't envy you sleeping there," he said, turning his gaze forward just in time to see a hundred gallons of dark green seawater burst into white foam inches from his face.

"I don't think where I'm sleeping is the problem," was my response after the wind had whisked the water away and the thunderous noise of the deluge had stopped.

"Your watch starts in twenty minutes," he said to the radar. "One thing about it, Mick. You don't have to go very far to get to work. Sure, you could almost do your watch without getting up out of bed."

"Yes, Hector, I probably could," I said, pulling on my clothes and haphazardly making haste to the head.

Alone in the galley with the pitching of the ship, concentrating on keeping my bowl and mug on the table, I ate my breakfast of peaches, cereal, toast and tea. Back on the bridge, braced against the table, a pencil dot marked our spot, one hundred and twenty-eight nautical miles out to sea.

"Steady as she goes, on 060," Hector said before leaving.

"Steady as she goes on 060," I echoed, taking control.

My watch passed quickly and without incident. For an hour, with a clean radar screen, it was just me and the sea and a scattered seabird that ghosted through the searchlight beam. I tried not to think too much.

<hr>

"Get up, Mick. The boys are getting ready to shoot the gear," I heard Ben say.

Coming awake, I sat up, dressed in the drab of predawn and headed to the head, then to the engine room. When I stepped through the door onto a wooden pallet placed outside the door on the shelter deck, the hatch covers of the fish hold were off. Under the floodlights in the rigging, I swayed to and fro and suited into my rubber clothes with the floodgates spewing seawater around my feet.

"You have never seen a fleet of gear being shot before, have you?" Jack asked me when I figured I was ready to go.

"No," I replied.

"Then stand close to me and do what I tell you."

"Roger."

With Ben at the helm, the dragger slowed down to about two knots. Jack and I stood on the port side. Todd and Don took up station across the way. In the hold, Greg passed the end of the mooring rope of fleet number one to Don, who in turn passed it to Hector standing by on the top deck. Hector tied three twenty-four-inch orange buoys to the rope and, one hundred and sixty nautical miles from Cape Chidley, he tossed the buoys over the side. "Floats gone!" he yelled at the bridge.

The dragger's speed increased and the bow swung northward. The mooring rope fed from the hold. On the bulkhead, next to the door, was mounted a camera with a microphone that displayed the entire sheltered deck area on a screen situated on the bridge. A similar one was mounted in the engine room. Greg kept Jack informed as to how much of the nine hundred fathoms of mooring rope remained. Jack, in turn, relayed this information to Ben at the helm by shouting at the microphone. The remaining end of the mooring rope was attached to the headrope of net number one. "A hundred fathoms!" Don shouted. The engine slowed to idle.

Hector arrived on the scene and stood up beside Jack and me. "Now, the rock must be tied on," Jack said to me. "Don and Todd will grab the net when it comes out of the hold. You and Hector grab the footrope and help them hold it while I make fast the rock."

The rock was a three-foot-long piece of railway iron that weighed nearly sixty pounds. It was called the rock because it was to sink the foot line of the net to rock bottom.

"Roger," I replied. Across the way Don and Todd got ready to grab the net.

"Ten fathoms!" Greg roared from the hold.

"Ten fathoms," Jack yelled at the camera.

I made ready and waited. As Hector and Todd grabbed for the net, I grabbed and held on for dear life. With speed and agility Jack tied on the rock. Lifting it in his arms, side by side we walked to the stern and he tossed it, destination rock bottom, 780 fathoms below.

"Rock's gone!" Jack bellowed, putting his arm across my chest and ushering me back out of the way. The dragger surged ahead.

Standing safely away we watched the net spew out. A few fathoms of webbing stayed afloat before it was dragged under. Here the seabirds swooped and flitted, fluttered and fought. One seagull, perhaps blinded by the glare of the lights, soared into the portion of the net between the ship and the sea. There was no escape. "Well, we'll have a seagull, anyway," I said to Jack sadly.

"No, we won't," he replied. "There won't be much left to it in a week's time. Let's hope some big, fat turbot eats him for breakfast."

"Ten nets!" Greg roared.

"Ten nets!" Jack bellowed. "Counting the knots as the nets leave the pounds tells us how many remain," he told me without me asking.

"Three nets!" The dragger slowed. "Get ready to grab the footrope when the boys grabs the headrope. Same as last time, I'll tie on the rock," Jack said leaning close to my ear.

"Roger."

"One net!" The dragger stopped. On cue, I grabbed the northern end of the fleet and held on tight. The crew grabbed the blue 5/8-inch mooring rope that Greg had fastened in the hold. Jack made fast the rock. With a motion of his head, we walked to the stern and he tossed the rock into the sea. "Nets gone!"

The mooring rope snaked over the stern and the dragger again picked up speed. On the top deck, Hector tied on three twenty-four-inch buoys and a "high-fly" reflector buoy to the remaining end of the mooring, and waited for its length to play out. High-fly buoys are made from a slender pole about ten feet in length. At the tip is fastened an aluminum reflector plate that the radar can detect in relatively calm seas. Halfway down, the pole passes through an eighteen-inch buoy. At the base of the pole is a twenty-pound concrete weight.

Hector tossed the floats over the side. "Floats gone!" he yelled at the bridge. The dragger picked up speed and Ben headed us to another coordinate fifteen miles distant. The gear was settling to the bottom. I had shot my first fleet.

"Nothing to it," Jack said as he shed the rubber gloves.

"Nothing to it," I repeated.

"It'll be almost a couple of hours before we set the next fleet. I'm going in for breakfast. Do you want two eggs or three?"

"Two will do, thank you," I replied.

Greg came up out of the hold with the end of mooring rope number two held in his hand. He passed the end up to Hector on the top deck and Hector tied it to the buoys. The next fleet was ready to shoot.

Everyone disappeared inside. Shedding my rubber clothes, I climbed the ladder through the hatch and stood on the top deck to watch what I knew was going to be a glorious dawn. Above the seas through which the *Styx* shouldered and sprayed, the darkness slowly surrendered to the light in a blaze of glory. There was no sign of the *Vantage*. It seemed as if we had the Labrador Sea all to ourselves.

At 5 p.m. seven fleets of gill nets totaling three miles of ten-inch monofilament webbing were set about the seafloor in between eight hundred and nine hundred fathoms of water, at seven different coordinates. Ben set a course for Port Burwell harbor.

At times, ship life is as routine as prison life, I figured, though I have never had the misfortune of being inside. It came down to the same faces, the same dinner times, the same supper times, the same menu, the same magazines, the same scenery, the same pace, the same smells. You meet in the galley, you brush past each other in the companionways. You wait at the washroom door, you see each other all about. You dirty the dishes, you wash the dishes, you boil the kettle, you take off the kettle. For some privacy I decided to see what it was like atop the wheelhouse.

I walked forward into the eye-watering wind and held onto a stay wire. The place was devoid of shelter. All that was up there was the radar housing and the searchlights. On the port side was the exhaust funnel that belched black clouds of thick oily smoke. Twenty feet up the spar a one-inch steel cable was stretched taut to the stem head. Two aluminum arms were welded there forming the stabilizer brackets. To these were mounted an array of fiberglass antennae, navigation lights and floodlights. Smaller steel cables were stretched taut to different parts of the ship. No railing surrounded this area.

Wednesday, September 2

IT WAS NOON BEFORE I HEARD "Land ho." The land was one of the Button Islands that are separated from Killiniq Island and Cape Chidley in the south by a narrow channel called the Grey Strait. Further south, the McClain Strait separated Killiniq Island from mainland Labrador. Ben chose a course that would bring us through the Grey Strait into the harbor of Port Burwell, situated on the island's west side. On the highest granite head, a dark rock figure, an Inukshuk, watched our approach, informing all that people have visited before. The tide was falling. On the shoreline the high water mark was etched into the rock face about twelve feet above the surface.

Ben gave orders to take in the fish, just before the bow of the *Styx* turned up the Grey Strait. The fast-moving current transformed the strait into a raging river. By the time we were abeam of the first of the Button Islands our speed had reduced to 3.2 knots. Ahead lay two miles of the same. Seals bobbed in the whirlpools, and seabirds dived and swam in the turmoil of it all.

Fighting for control in midstream, Ben didn't say much other than, "Idden't this wicked!" His eyes were glued to the windows; his hands constantly spun the steering wheel to maintain control. The speed indicator displayed 1.2 knots. We were hardly making headway.

"This is not a nice place to lose power," Wayne commented.

"Piece of ice coming there!" Greg exclaimed.

The warning of growlers killed all conversation and sent a shiver through me. Huddled together on the bridge, we watched in silence as the fragment of certain devastation plunged and rolled, hissed and swirled its way closer and closer to our frail hull. At two hundred yards the growler shone a deadly aquagreen. Momentum lifted it up and gravity pulled it back down. The tortured tide pull spun it around and around. Then the growler disappeared. No one was certain where it would resurface, though we all knew it would.

"There it is!" Greg cried suddenly, pointing to a spot off to starboard. Within an instant, the ship was sucked into a massive whirlpool. We were all thrown to port. Ben compensated by spinning the wheel to turn the bow back on course. Slowly the bow responded. Ben regained some control and the growler hissed by the hull. I estimated the size of the small piece of iceberg to be as large as two Lincoln Continentals and a thousand times harder. Ahead for another mile the waters raged.

Without warning the bow dropped out of sight as if we had dropped off the edge of the earth. Water spattered the windows as hard as it had at any time we punched it out at sea. Ben fought for control. I almost fell out of the seat. The hull pulled itself out, hesitantly responded to the rudder and settled haphazardly back on course. The tides begrudgingly gave us headway. Fifty intense minutes later we rounded the point and the *Bakur* came into view, all hands on deck.

"Bakur" is a Norwegian word meaning shark. Sharks are caught using trawls, consisting of a series of baited hooks fastened at specific intervals to a moored headrope. The trawl is pulled from the ocean floor by a gurdy and the catch is cleaned and stowed in the hold. At present the *Bakur* was fitted for receiving, processing and blast-freezing the turbot that we hoped were filling up our nets. Approaching slowly, I made ready with the bowline. There was no trouble to get someone to catch it because there were men everywhere.

Just before the fenders squeezed between the two steel hulls, I tossed the bowline to an eager young man with a bald head. In just a few minutes we were tied up broadside and the air was buzzing with eager voices.

Ben spoke to the skipper through the windows, bridge to bridge, about the tides in the strait. "Never before have I seen such a hellish place. It was like steaming up the Gander River during the spring runoff."

Jack asked someone else, "How's it going?"

Above the din, a voice eagerly asked, "Do you have any packages aboard for us?"

"Mick, come give me a hand," Todd said.

Following him astern to the deepest recesses of the hold, through a rusty watertight steel door in the rear center pound, we went for the packages. In the rudder compartment, laid on the five-gallon cans of engine oil and gasoline, were two boxes with the Player's emblem on them.

The smell of oil in the damp space was overpowering. Todd passed me a box. He grabbed the remaining one. "These cigarettes won't be fit to smoke," I thought, as I made my way back through the hold and up the ladder to the shelter deck. It seemed all eyes were on me when I broke into view. Eager hands stretched out to relieve me of my burden. Suddenly, the deck was deserted except for a few stragglers. After a few minutes the men reappeared on deck smoking. One fellow had a lighted cigarette in his mouth and a cigarette behind each ear. Sporadic coughing mixed in with the conversations.

The *Bakur* was home for twenty-four men. A regular crew of eight, and sixteen men to process the turbot. Also aboard was a representative from a Japanese fish-buying company, Kim, who intended to pay eighty cents for each and every pound of number one turbot that was blast-frozen in the *Bakur*'s freezers.

The next three hours were spent refueling, topping up our water tanks and making good use of the *Bakur*'s washer and dryer. The bald-headed guy invited me to come aboard for coffee. Eager for a change of company, I introduced myself and hopped aboard. He told me his name was Jim. "Want a cup of tea?" he asked.

"Yes, that would be fine."

The galley was located aft below the wheelhouse. Eight men, most of them smoking, sat around one of the two galley tables. They drank tea and watched an action movie on the wall-mounted television. I sat at the table next to a big man wearing an earring and sporting a ponytail. "How's it going? I'm Mick."

"Best kind," he replied through a thick cloud of smoke. "I'm Reg, how's it going with you?"

"Not bad," I replied, settling in beside him.

"Want some lemon pie?" Reg asked.

"Yes, I'd love some."

Promptly a large lemon meringue pie was placed on the table in front of me, along with a knife, a fork and a plate. "Help yourself."

Feeling right at home, I dug into the tasty treat. "Want some ice cream with that?" Reg asked.

"No, thanks. Maybe with the next piece." In the short time spent aboard I acquired a lot of information from talking and listening to the men, including the captain who came in for coffee.

"This is Captain Kirk, and you're on the turbot ship, *Bakur*," Jim introduced him with a chuckle.

He was a curly-headed, middle-aged man with a friendly face. "Welcome aboard," he said.

"Thank you, sir."

Most of the turbot men were from the Northern Peninsula, St. Anthony area. Jim was from L'Anse aux Meadows, while a few fellows hailed from Fox Harbour and Mary's Harbour located in southern Labrador.

According to reports there was no longer a Port Burwell. All that was left of it was a few concrete foundations. The hub of the area was a place called Mission Harbour, located on the southern side of McGregor Strait about three miles away by boat. A once thriving town, it was the northernmost town in Labrador and had boasted almost two hundred Inuit residents. The federal government had built a fish plant with freezing capabilities geared towards the processing of arctic char. But the supply of char did not meet demands and the fish plant was shut down. The place was then abandoned. The residents moved to Kangiqsualujjuaq, located on the shore of Ungava Bay, one hundred and fifty miles to the south. All that remained in Mission Harbour was a refueling station for helicopters, a high steel transmission/communication tower and a few buildings that had not yet blown away. Presently, the town was inhabited by a group of fifteen Inuit. Some of them were staying aboard a thirty-five-foot-long liner that was moored in the harbor. During the summer months the federal government employed the people who once lived there to demolish some of the buildings.

"Have you seen any polar bears?" I asked Jim.

"Yes, we see them all the time in on the hills and out in the landwash. Some brutes, too. When the skipper sends us ashore for water, he won't let us go without a gun. This is no place to be ashore unarmed," he replied.

"I've never seen a live, wild polar bear," I said.

"Well, they're alive enough around here. It won't be long before you see one, maybe two or three," Reg commented.

"Have another cup of tea and a bun," the cook said, poking his head out through the dumbwaiter in the galley.

"Don't mind if I do, thank you." The place started to fill up. Some talked, some listened, some watched, others ate and sipped tea. Most everyone smoked.

"What kind of a time did you have comin' up the coast?" Jim asked, ignoring the blaring set and looking directly at me.

"Weather-wise, it was the best kind. We spent a night in a fjord out of the wind, but that was more to keep the *Vantage* company than anything else," I replied.

"We've been here idle for the last thirteen days," he said. "We've been five days without smokes."

"What about pay?" I asked.

"We get paid ninety dollars every day," Jim replied. "If it was any other way no one would stay."

"What are the onboard accommodations like?"

"Number one. The cook serves up three square meals a day whether you wants it or not. Lying around waiting is the worst of it," Jim told me. "It's boring; not a thing to do but eat and lie around. To tell the truth, these days the toilet works the hardest aboard this one."

"I hope we can change that in a few days when we get back from the gear," I said.

"Yes, boy, it'd be alright. Try to come in on Friday nights."

"Why?" I asked.

"Because we get paid time and a half if we work during the weekend. Although if it weren't for the calendar, I wouldn't know one day from the other."

Just as I finished eating, Todd came in the galley and informed all that the *Styx* was heading for anchorage. The galley emptied.

Chilly westerlies whisked by me on the bow of the *Styx* as I waited to receive the order from Ben to let go the bowline. I gave the *Bakur* the once-over.

She was spotless. Against the aft superstructure was an immense ice-making machine covered with a blue tarpaulin. Before sailing out to the fishing grounds, we'd be back to get an ample supply to ice down our catch.

The sheltered bow area was geared up as a mini-fish plant. A steel ladder led up to where Jim stood. Just behind him, covered with tarpaulins, hundreds of white trays were neatly stacked, with ample room allocated for the anchor winch.

"Let go the bowline!" Ben shouted from the bridge.

For anchorage, Ben chose a cove gouged into the side of Killiniq Island about a mile from the *Bakur*. The steel doors hadn't reached the bottom before Greg and Todd were out with their guns on alert for flybys.

With the *Styx* anchored from the stern, she lay stern on to the wind, and from the vantage point of my crab pot, I had an unobstructed view of the terrain to the north. I tried to ignore the sounds Greg and Todd made as they tried their aim on the bow and concentrated my attention on scanning for my first sighting of a live polar bear in its natural habitat.

Killiniq Island lay about three hundred yards astern. The tide had dropped halfway. Above and beyond the shore, there was not a single color shrub to be seen, much less a tree. I'd have bet that had I released a healthy woodpecker, it would have collapsed onto the tundra from exhaustion before finding a branch big enough to rest upon. No tall grass bent in the wind. No birds sang.

The most predominant color was the green of the tundra. What wasn't green loomed up granite gray. In the haze to the south and west, the low foothills rolled and rose higher and higher like loaves of homemade bread. Some were glazed with gray cloud cover. Above that everything was gray.

To the east the shoreline was shattered in places by what appeared to be a backbone. Huge rocks of all shapes and sizes stretched from the face of the high slope down into the sea. Immense boulder beds, rubble pits and scree slopes scarred the area. Strewn about the tundra-covered slopes, sometimes silhouetted against the sky, lay huge granite boulders, droppings of the receding glaciers. In a shaded gorge lay a drift of snow, the only bright spot to be seen.

Todd walked up beside me with the shotgun and asked, "Do you want a shot?"

"Sure," I replied.

He passed me the gun and showed me where the safety was. "She's fully loaded," he said.

Shouldering it, I pointed the bead into the sky and pulled the trigger as fast as the mechanism would allow me. The gun recoiled five times and five spent shells ejected over the side. I passed the gun back to him. "Thanks."

"What did you shoot at?" he asked, somewhat surprised.

"The sky. What did you think I was going to shoot at?" I replied.

"I thought you might shoot a bird."

"I don't shoot birds in waste anymore, boy," I replied, looking him straight in the eye. "I gave it up a long time ago after a fellow said something that changed my attitude."

"What did he say to you?" he inquired, seemingly interested.

"He said, 'Stop needlessly shooting birds and living things. You never know. When you have gasped your last breath, you may return as a bird and someone will blast you out of the sky for no reason. It may be that you will have a broken wing. You might live to die a long, lingering death.' I never shot things in waste after that."

"Ben don't care," came his weak defense.

"You should care," I said.

"Todd, come here and have a look at this," Greg called from the bow.

Todd turned away without speaking. I went below thinking that he was five shells closer to being out of ammo, if nothing else.

After supper a few of the crew congregated on the bridge to chew the fat, scan the terrain, listen to Don trying to play the guitar and hear the marine weather forecast.

Todd brought up the topic of pillaging the town of Mission Harbour. "The place is abandoned. The Inuit are tearing it down. Nobody owns it. No one knows what we could find in there," he said with a gleam in his eye.

"I'll be looking for some angle iron to bring home to make a trailer," Don added with relish.

Ben was slouched in the commander's chair picking his teeth with a toothpick. His attention seemed out the window.

Alone in the roomy rumble seat, taking it all in, it didn't surprise me that the captain did not put a halt to the plans being made to pillage the town. My own interest in going ashore was to get a change of scenery, stretch my legs and maybe find a lonely spot to sit for a while. From the looks of the terrain, all one had to do was pick a spot to sit. Maybe I'd stumble across an ivory carving that some old Inuit hunter had lost along the way.

"What about you, Mick?" Don asked. "Do you need any angle iron?"

"No, I can't say I do. I have a brother-in-law who is a welder and he has truckloads of angle iron over there. Thanks anyway," I replied.

The lights of the *Vantage* glowed like a constellation as Jerry steamed into Port Burwell under the cover of darkness. Ben radioed Jerry and was told that all six fleets were fishing. Refueling and replenishing water tanks would wait until tomorrow. What seemed to be a weary voice related a rush of an experience in the strait and by the sound of the tinny voice that filled the bridge, he seemed glad to be in port.

After they signed off, another voice over the radio filled the bridge wall to wall: "All stations, all stations … Iqaluit Coast Guard Radio, with the marine weather forecast for tonight and Thursday as issued by Environment Canada … for Cape Chidley, light westerlies tonight, shifting to light northerlies early in the evening. Snow accumulation five centimeters. Clearing in the evening. Low overnight -4°C, high tomorrow 6°C."

Thursday, September 3

AT MIDNIGHT, IT WAS SOFTLY SNOWING in Port Burwell. The *Styx* wore a three-inch-thick cloak of it. Before climbing inside my sleeping bag, I fished a pair of long underwear and a T-shirt from my clothes bag and pulled them on. The thought of the thick eiderdown on my own bed at home and my warm wife curled up all alone beneath its warmth made me homesick.

~~~~~~~~~~~~~~~~~~~~~~~~~~~~~~

The grinding sound of the toilet water pump awakened me the next morning. Opening my eyes, the first thing I saw was my breath. All forward windows sported a drift of snow that crept six inches up the glass.

From below arose the sounds of pots banging and cupboard doors opening and closing. The *Styx* was coming to life. The enticing smell of frying bacon prompted me to sit up and meet the morning.

Through every bridge window the view was the same: green, white and gray. The snow had stopped falling. The tide was high. The sea was flecked with whitecaps. The Labrador wilds were white. The cloud cover appeared to be lifting and softening, lightened by the loss of snow, but not a pinprick of sunshine peeped through. The blue hull of the *Vantage* anchored a mile away stood out, while the black and white of the *Bakur* blended in perfectly with the seascape.

From below the activity intensified. Sneakered feet climbed the steps up to the bridge two at a time. It was Todd, apparently in good spirits. "You going ashore?" he asked with excitement and expectation in his voice.

I wasn't that eager to go. A part of me didn't want to see. "I'm not sure," I replied.

Todd opened the top half of the port-side door and the wind invaded the bridge. As he scanned, he said encouragingly, "Come ashore with us when we go. You'll get a chance to stretch your legs on the tip of the Labrador. You never know when you'll have another chance. We might see a polar bear."

"Who is going ashore with you?"
~~~~~~~~~~~~~~~~~~~~~~~~~~~~~~

The gunwale of the speedboat wasn't six inches above the water by the time Todd, Don, Greg, Ben and I settled aboard to begin the twenty-minute spin to Mission Harbour. Glen gunned the engine south towards a rocky point, then east into the channel that made Killiniq an island. The town, constructed on the south side of the channel, came into view.

On approach, the first building was the fish plant. We tied the speedboat to a stage made of long poles and flat boards that clung to the shore fifty feet from the fish-plant door.

I was excited. For the first time in my life I was in polar bear territory. An encounter could be expected at anytime. One weighing a thousand pounds might be lurking inside that door. I wasn't the least bit apprehensive or afraid.

The plant doors opened into a wide room that contained nothing more than the remains of a stainless steel cutting table and a nylon net. A side door opened into another, even larger room containing about one hundred bags of salt and a few metal pound boards. Up in a corner rested the rusted skeleton of a wheelbarrow. Next to the exit door, stapled on the wall, was a sign printed in English, French and Inuktitut that read:

NOTICE TO ALL VISITORS TO KILLINIQ

We, the Inuit of Killiniq, were forced to abandon our community on Killiniq Island in 1978. Many of us now live in Kangiqsualujjuaq but still return to hunt and fish on the island. Since the community was abandoned some visitors have broken and damaged the buildings that are left and have shown little respect for the environment.

In 1995 Inuit from the Killiniq families and Makivik Corporation, which represents the Inuit of Nunavik, began a cleanup of the abandoned community site. We were assisted by the Department of Indian and Northern Affairs and the Canadian Coast Guard. We have only begun the cleanup and hope to continue in future years.

We ask all visitors to respect the environs around Killiniq and the work we have started. If you use the buildings, please close them. Do not damage them anymore. Put any garbage in the new dump up on the hill past the old church. Please keep the place clean for everybody's sake.

With a preliminary inspection of the fishless plant complete, we went outside in single file. Thirty feet in front of us was a small boat haul-up constructed of telephone poles. Around the corner several smaller outbuildings were attached to the fish plant. One housed the cannibalized remains of the refrigeration units that were, according to Don, "of no use to us." The office area was ransacked. A few tally sheets littered the floor. In the last attached building lay the remains of a urinal. Underneath this section of the building Don spotted some angle iron. "I just found my trailer," he said delightedly. On bended knee he inspected his discovery: six lengths of two-inch angle iron, about fifty feet total. The iron looked new. "Just what the doctor ordered," he said, pleased as punch.

"There's almost enough there to make a trailer for me, too, Don," Ben said, looking at the iron.

"Yes, there is, and this might not be all the iron that's around," Don replied. Before straightening up, he pushed the iron back beneath the building.

"Look at the fiberglass antennae poles over here," Greg shouted from somewhere behind the plant.

"Where?" Ben blared back. "What kind of antennae poles?"

By the time we made our way over Greg had the four

antennae laid on the ground. Each was two inches in diameter and thirty feet long, individually wrapped in cardboard. Ben seemed to be watching the terrain more than the booty. Barely glancing at the antennae, he said, "Nice to know they're there."

After we had fully explored the buildings, we gathered to walk along a path up a steep hill. Spaced at regular intervals along the path were culvert pipes, four feet high and six feet in diameter. Sticking up like sore thumbs through the stones that filled them were the stumps of telephone poles.

At the summit we had a commanding view of the channel and Mission Harbour huddled in the cove below. The most striking feature was the colors of the wooden buildings. The yellows, blues and greens of the dozen single-story dwellings stood in vivid contrast to the snow-covered terrain. From west to east a channel flowed past the fish-plant wharf, before emptying into the sea. Killiniq Island bounded the north shore of the channel that in one place narrowed to less than one hundred yards where a huge boulder bed tumbled into the channel. With the tide falling, fast water rapids began to form.

On the highest rounded summit three Inukshuk stood silhouetted against the skyline, watching down over the town like vigilant sentries.

A wooden long-liner lay at anchor in the cove. All about the deck were the former residents of Mission Harbour: women and children, men and dogs. Some stood and stared at us. The dogs barked. Two speedboats fitted with outboard motors were tied to the stern.

With the tide dropping, Ben became concerned about the speedboat. "Don, you and Todd go back and bring the boat around to the slip and pull her in. We'll wait for you here," he said.

Mission Harbour seemed a bleak, desolate place of residence. And that was on a good day. A shiver passed through me as I thought of standing here on a blustery day in February.

Most of the colored buildings were perched in the lee of the height on which we stood. Several of the buildings were mobile homes. Steel cables anchored into the granite kept them from blowing away.

A one-hundred-foot steel tower overlooked Mission Harbour. Below that stood two rusty fuel storage tanks. A rusty six-inch pipe supported at intervals with iron drums filled with rock and cement led from the base of one fuel tank down the hill towards the fish plant. A similar pipe snaked from the other fuel tank, past the heli-pad and down into town. The heli-pad looked well maintained and brightly painted. Near at hand and neatly stacked were about fifty fuel drums.

The church mentioned on the notice stapled to the fish-plant wall was off by itself about a half-mile away. The single-story structure appeared to be cuddled in a hollow in the lee of a rock outcrop. With snow covering the ground it reminded me of a Christmas postcard. The roof had a gaping hole in it as if the fist of God had crashed through it. Further up the hill past the church was the dump.

Don and Todd trudged up the hill, puffing and blowing. "All secure, skipper," Don reported. In single file with guns at the ready, Ben led us into town.

The wooden houses were shacks. The two dwellings that seemed livable were locked. The other buildings amounted to nothing more than kindling. Inside them, other than squalor, we found a foul odor. "Must be the dog's house," Todd commented.

The trailers with stovepipes stuck through the windows were in even worse shape. The two structures that seemed sound were the steel generator building and an adjoining workshop.

The generator building was about the same size as the fish plant, with a fifteen-foot ceiling and a large folding garage door. A ten-foot-wide strip of metal roofing was missing, probably blown away. Inside, mounted to the concrete floor, were two diesel generators in a sad state of repair. Don inspected them right away.

"Anything on them that's of use to us, I wonder?" he said more to himself than to anyone in particular.

We spread out to see what could be found. Shelves and bins were built on a wall and in some of the bins Greg found an assortment of fittings. One bin contained electrical conduit connectors. "I'm taking some of them for the boat," he said decisively.

"Don't take anything yet. Not while the Eskimos are here. We'll be back again. Before we leave to go home we'll bring it aboard," said Ben.

An old hot air furnace hung from the ceiling with the duct work attached. In the corner stood some empty fuel tanks.

We were aware of the Inuit watching us. Grouped together we continued along the winding trail towards the next place of interest, the dump. I was expecting to see a polar bear at any step.

Amid the rubble in the dump, the first thing to catch the eye was a J-5 tractor with a trailer hooked up to it. Don climbed aboard, sat in the seat and started to pull on the levers. "Any way of getting this aboard the *Styx*, Ben?" he asked.

"I don't think so," Ben replied.

Evidently, the cleanup of the town meant ripping the buildings to pieces, loading the material on the trailer and pulling it up here with the tractor where it was dumped, doused with fuel and set afire. Spread all about over a fifty-square-yard area lay charred metal paneling, steel beams, about one hundred 45-gallon steel drums, large propane tanks and snarls of wire. Todd picked up a piece of the wire and examined it. "Too bad it's not copper," he said. "If it was, we'd bring back a load of scrap."

"If it was copper, it wouldn't be here," Don said smartly.

"No, you're probably right, someone else would have taken it by now."

"I'm looking for a ball joint for my old Chevy pickup," I said. "If you sees one let me know."

"I don't say there's a ball joint within five hundred miles," Don replied.

The church caught my attention. Without saying anything I left them to rummage and walked over. It was easy to enter through a hole in the rear. Whatever had crashed through the roof looked like it had exited through the rear and had blasted out all the windows. The floor was strewn with pieces of framework and glass fragments. The place was empty of chairs and furniture. I took off my hat and went inside to say my prayers. Ten Hail Marys or so later Todd and Greg barged in like they did when entering any other building. It didn't take them long to satisfy their curiosity and they left again. A few minutes later I finished my devotions and followed them back down the hill.

The heli-pad grabbed Ben's attention next. No sooner were we gathered on the flat wooden deck when the sound of a helicopter caught our attention. It wasn't long before it came into view, heading directly towards us.

"Put away the guns, boys," Ben said, passing his rifle to Greg. Greg and Tod hid their guns behind the fuel drums.

The pilot landed in a whirlwind. After the rotor stopped spinning, we approached as a young man got out. In a distinct French accent he asked, "Where are your guns?"

No one replied.

"You shouldn't be traveling without a gun. There are polar bears around here that will eat you up. By the way, my name is Jacques."

Somewhat sheepishly, we introduced ourselves. Jacques rolled a fuel drum up beside the helicopter and tore off the seal.

While he was refueling we learned that he was flying to Goose Bay from Iqaluit. "A long flight," he described it. In less than thirty minutes, after farewell waves and good wishes, Jacques was on his way again.

The sound of an outboard motor carried on the wind. A speedboat with four occupants sped across the cove to a finger of land below a round rocky head, where they stopped and jumped out. Gathering up the guns, Ben suggested, "Let's go over and see what's happening."

The group was made up of an older Inuit man and three boys. The old man held an ancient radio. The boys unwound a wire and stretched it out up the face of the bluff. As soon as we approached, the old man asked, "Cigarettes?"

Nodding my head and smiling, I took out my pack and offered him one. A broad smile of contentment lit his face as he exhaled a mighty lungful of smoke. Lighting one myself I passed them around. Shortly, we were smiling and blowing smoke into the chilly breeze.

They didn't seem a bit cold with their bare hands and heads, and wide-open coats and shirts with buttons undone and Adam's apples exposed. The lads remained quiet while Ben questioned the old man. Apparently work demolishing the town was finished for the summer. Soon they would be traveling back to Kangiqsualujjuaq one hundred and fifty miles south on the eastern shore of Ungava Bay. Into a radio transmitter, he spoke in his native tongue. Presently, the squawk box emitted a tinny, distant female voice and all listened anxiously. After a few short exchanges, he put down the receiver and the lads coiled up the antenna wire. "Cigarette?" he asked with a wrinkled grin. I handed out another round.

"Polar bears around here?" Ben asked.

The old man nodded. "Few, later we come back on snowmobiles to kill them."

"Geese?" Ben inquired.

The man glanced at the ground and shook his head. "Not many. All gone south."

"Caribou?"

"Perhaps," was the reply.

"There's lots of seals here," Todd volunteered.

"Yes," he nodded. "Plenty seals."

"Char?" Greg asked.

"Mmmm. Not many. Five days ago we caught one and a walrus. Cigarette?" he asked, looking at me.

Taking the pack from my pocket, I extracted a couple of cigarettes to keep for myself and handed him the rest. He lit one immediately and put the remainder inside his shirt. With a broad grin, he turned away and the four of them jumped aboard the boat and sped back to the long-liner, leaving us on the barren height and no wiser about their radio conversation.

With our tour of the town completed, we meandered back to the boat. To get it afloat, we lifted it up and carried it fifty feet to the water. We clambered aboard. Everyone was eager to get back to the heat of the galley, hot tea and food. As we left the town in our wake, I was disappointed not to have made my first sighting of a polar bear, yet I had a strange feeling that one had sighted me.

The *Vantage* was tied up to the port side of the *Styx* when we climbed aboard. After a hearty supper cooked by Wayne, I went aboard the *Vantage* for a visit. She carried a full contingent of eight. I knew most of them from previous sealing expeditions.

The galley of the *Styx* was spacious compared to the galley on the *Vantage*. Like sardines we crammed together for an hour or more, sipping tea, exchanging stories, laughing and carrying on. None of this crew had ever fished this far from home. We speculated how cramped it must be on those turbot fishing vessels that carried two crews in order to work around the clock. One crew slept as the other worked. It must be awful when the vessel was steaming or when they were unable to work the gear in bad weather. During those times one crew slept in the galley. All agreed that everybody earned their meager share on those vessels.

A few of the *Vantage's* crew members wanted to know what was left in Mission Harbour. I told them what I had encountered. Some of them seemed eager to go look for themselves.

A little later we heard the sound of an outboard motor and scurried to see what was happening. Close to the rail was one of the speedboats we had seen in the harbor. A stocky, middle-aged man stood backed by a forty-horsepower Honda engine. A woman covered in caribou hides and holding a small child in her arms sat directly in front of him. Two youngsters, maybe eight and ten years old, sat amidships beside an old stove. A large husky and a teenage boy occupied the bow. Beside the boy was a rifle.

"Cigarettes?" the Inuit man asked with a hopeful grin on his weather-beaten face. I passed him down four or five. He passed one to the woman and they lit up immediately. Todd went inside and brought out a couple of chocolate bars and some candy. He passed the sweets to one of the young children and her round face lit up into a big smile. She put one candy in her mouth and the rest inside her coat. A second speedboat holding four other occupants and a dog idled fifty yards away. We learned that they were leaving for the winter. Kangiqsualujjuaq was their destination. Looking at them sitting there in the small open boat, comfortable and seemingly having no fear of the long trek ahead of them, I asked, "Where will you stay the night?"

"Somewhere," was the man's reply and, placing the motor in gear, he nodded and waved goodbye as they sped away across the bay. The white tips of the waves, the white hulls and the driving spray blended them in perfectly and they vanished from my view.

<hr>

At 5 p.m. Captain Kirk radioed over to inform Ben that our ice was ready. We slipped the lines, pulled in the doors and cruised over, tying up to the *Bakur*. The *Vantage* tied up to the *Bakur*'s other side. The turbot men loaded the ice into our center pound by forming a long procession. From hand to hand they passed the ice-filled trays from their deck to ours before emptying them one at a time into our hold. They appeared to be a jolly group and in just over an hour they were done. Then they started on the *Vantage*. By 7 p.m. all the decks were quiet. The washer and dryer worked time and a half. We were ready and rearing to go out to the fishing ground to retrieve fifty thousand pounds of number one turbot that I hoped was entangled in our nets.

Greg had brought aboard an action movie that one of the men on the *Bakur* lent him, and he played it on the VCR. Wayne watched and seemed not to mind the bombing, shooting and noisy scenes. The terrified screams of the scantily clad females seemed not to distress him a bit. However, as soon as he heard the word "Goddamn," he jumped up and blurted, "Turn that off, boys! Turn it off! I'm not having that language on this boat!" Greg switched off the television and ejected the cassette. Under heavy eyebrows, he disappeared into his room and closed the door firmly behind him. I left the galley with my cup of tea in hand, craving nicotine.

The harbor had become a bit choppy and both the *Styx* and the *Vantage* rolled around a lot, making things uncomfortable. At 10 p.m. Ben gave orders to slip the lines and we cruised back to drop the doors at our previous anchorage. The navigation lights of the *Bakur* and *Vantage* reflected across the water. It began to snow again and by midnight, when I last looked out through the windows, about an inch of fluff had nestled on the sills.

Friday, September 4

CONFINED TO THE SHIP FOR THE NEXT FEW DAYS, we did what crews do when waiting. We slept, sat around, rewatched revivals and hockey games. We soiled the dishes, we cleaned the dishes. We reread magazines. We rose up and down with the tide and swung to and fro on the end of the cables.

After the Inuit long-liner steamed out of Mission Harbour, bound for Ungava Bay with all the remaining inhabitants, Jerry shifted the *Vantage* to take up anchorage in the spot now vacated. The *Styx* could pass through the strait only at high tide.

For a short spell the winds dropped enough for Greg, Don, Todd, Hector and me to go into Mission Harbour in the speed-boat. Don was uneasy about his angle iron, suspecting that one of the *Vantage* crew might steal it away from him. I still hoped to see a polar bear.

Don's iron was as he had left it. Upon approach to the generator building, we encountered a monstrous male polar bear. From the top of the building we watched the nonthreatening beast feed on the entrails of the walrus the Inuit had killed. The boys drove him off with the guns, playing the game, "See-who-can-come-the-closest."

Saturday, September 5

ONE A.M. FOUND ME WRAPPED UP in my sleeping bag on the bridge of a deathly quiet ship. According to the forecast, the northerly winds were to diminish and the weather looked good for fishing for the following few days. Ben advised that we'd be sailing for the fishing grounds on the evening tide that next day, giving us ample sailing time to arrive at the coordinates of fleet number one around dawn.

I hardly knew what to expect. The crew expected enough fish for fifteen thousand dollars. I had no idea what kind of work was involved in this monetary gain, but my suspicions were that it didn't come easy. Nothing about fishing is easy. Some types of fishing are more rewarding, and less labor intensive and dangerous than others, but none of them are easy.

The physical part didn't keep me awake. I have sealed and am convinced that no type of fishing is worse than sealing. To me, sealing is the epitome of modern-day slavery. Nothing is worse than sealing.

Hector had said that it wasn't unusual for this crew to pull, pick and reset three fleets a day when weather conditions were good. We could be back in a week with fifty thousand pounds of turbot. At eighty cents per pound, that totaled forty thousand dollars. Six percent of forty thousand dollars came to twenty-four hundred dollars. This excited me. To make twenty-four hundred dollars sealing, the crew had to find, get in range of, shoot, retrieve, butcher, pelt, wash, shift, stow, shift, count, shift, stow, ice and discharge twenty-four hundred harps and their body parts.

The best day ever tallied for sealing on the *Vantage* was just shy of five hundred. To earn the same share meant five days of slave labor, not to mention the dangers of working in an arctic ice field. The thought opened wide my eyes and I spied the moon. I had to get up to look.

I swung open the top half of the starboard door and let the night flood in. Across the bay, a nautical mile away, the lights of the *Bakur* glowed in the night. The sky was streaked with jet tracks and studded with glittering stars. Aurora borealis claimed the northern quadrant as a dance floor where colored streaks shifted and swirled. Tongues of blue flared like burning propane. Ribbons of orange leapt like flames. Bands of light burned ten shades of red. The Big Dipper spilled out the boundless beauty of the Milky Way. In an instant I realized how and why a human being could love such a desolate, lonely place.

"Coming ashore with me, Mick?" I heard Don say.

Roused from my sleep, I opened my eyes to see Don and Greg on the bridge. "What?"

"Let's get ready and go to Mission Harbour. I kind of thinks the boys will take my angle iron. I wouldn't mind taking another stroll to the dump before we leaves for the fishing grounds."

"Sure, I'll go with you. It's a beautiful morning for a walk," I answered, looking past Greg to the snow-covered hills above the mirror-smooth waters of the bay. The wind had blown most of the snow off the cliffs close to shore. The snow-filled cracks and crevices showed up like wrinkles on aged faces.

As soon as Don, Jack, Todd, Greg and I rounded the point, we spotted a male polar bear feasting on a seal in the landwash. Against the brown color of the beach the beast looked like a piece of ice. "Look there!" said Jack, easing back on the throttle. The ice bear looked at us. Even from this safe distance I was intimidated.

"He must be a thousand pounds," Todd declared with awe in his voice.

"Yes, my son, every bit," confirmed Jack. The outboard stuttered and shut down. The intimidation feeling increased. A hush fell over us.

The bear dropped his stare. With the eighty-pound seal gripped between its teeth, he turned away from us and without pausing or looking back, he dragged his feast to the crest of the four-hundred-foot bluff. There he stopped, dropped the seal and looked back down at us.

Greg raised his rifle. "Don't you shoot that bear, Greg!" Jack warned.

"I'm not going to shoot," he replied with the scope to his eye.

"You better not! We don't need a wounded polar bear on the loose around here."

The bear bit into his feast and disappeared over the hill.

Jack pulled on the starter cord about a dozen times rapidly in succession before the outboard fired to life. When we landed at the fish plant, Dave of the *Vantage*, wearing coveralls and sneakers, was busy enough to break a sweat unscrewing the brackets that hung the folding doors. "What are you doing?" I asked.

Stopping, he replied, "Getting these doors ready for shipment. They're going to be hanging in my garage in a couple months' time, boy," he said, patting the door approvingly.

Personally, I didn't care if he disassembled the building and brought it back. "Are you sure they'll fit?"

"Yes, like a smack in the mouth," he replied. "If they don't, I'll make them fit," he said, resuming his work.

Without preliminaries, Don asked distrustfully, "Anybody take my angle iron?"

"I don't know anything about angle iron. Where is it?"

"Up under the building."

"Well then, it's still there, unless one of the boys took it."

"It better be there!"

Don pulled the angle iron out from under the outbuilding and wrote his name on each length with a marker. He also marked Ben's name on two of the fiberglass antennae.

I told Dave about the bear dragging the seal up and over the steep hill. "Yes, I bet the same bear watched us for over an hour just after daylight. Gerald heard him scratching at the hull. He rubbed the hull all the way round with his fur. I could have scratched his back. That's not the only one that's around, either. A mother bear and her two cubs sniffed around for a spell after the big fellow left. The cubs are about three hundred pounds. Gerald filmed them with the video."

"Not a nice thing to meet in the dark," I ventured.

"Not a nice thing to meet at any time," he declared.

After leaving him to his demolition duties, Don and I followed the enormous bear tracks up the steep grade and down into town. Greg found an unopened tin of welding rods under a bench in the generator building and placed them outside to bring aboard. Then it was on to the dump. With eyes peeled for polar bears, we plodded up the grade.

During the time the others took to forage, I visited the church. By this time tomorrow we'd be getting well out into the guts of the Labrador Sea. The three Inukshuk watched it all.

A foreboding befell me. I suspected it was because of the horrific way the crew treated the creatures. I reflected back to one barbaric event that happened one sunny day when I was a boy of seven, nestled in the bow of my father's passenger boat watching the stem break the blue waves to white foam. It was my favorite place on the entire boat. In the surge of the stem just behind my reflection, I spotted big fish swimming just beneath the water, almost touching us. Amazed, I watched them, and suddenly they jumped out of the water right in front of me.

"Dad! Dad! There's flying fish in the water up here!" I yelled excitedly at the wheelhouse where my father stood at the helm.

Glancing at the sea, he replied, "That's porpoises. Come here and take the wheel."

Reluctantly, I dragged myself aft. I wanted to see the flying fish. He overturned a wooden crate in front of the wheel for me to stand on. "Steer for that hill."

I followed orders. Dad produced a single-barrel shotgun from underneath the bench. Opening a drawer, he fished a shell and loaded it. From the wheelhouse to the bow he walked. There he took calculated aim. Boom! What a fright I got. I almost fell off the crate. "See if you can see him in the wake!" Dad shouted.

"Why did you shoot the flying fish?" I asked when he came back inside and put away the gun.

"Because!" he said, resuming control.

I bolted from the wheelhouse and ran to the stern where I searched for them in the wake. They were nowhere to be seen. I ran to the bow. All the flying fish were gone. I ran back to the stern to look again. Not a single flying fish to be seen. Out loud, I made a promise to them that if they did come back to play, I wouldn't tell my father. That incident played on my mind for a long time and haunted many of my nights. It began the path that led me away from the thoughtless cruelty of many of my fellow islanders who lived from the sea. It is a difficult divide to carry in your soul—that you must kill creatures to eke out a living and yet respect then enough not to kill them for sport or pleasure alone.

"You ready to go?" Don asked, poking his head in through a broken window frame.

Somewhat reluctantly I replied, "Yes, lead on, Don."

〜〜〜〜〜〜〜〜〜〜〜〜〜〜〜〜

After the feast of spaghetti and meatballs around noon there wasn't much room at the galley table. I wasn't complaining. For dessert, Jack had baked two delicious apple pies. "Good pie, Mickey?" he inquired, as I indulged.

"Excellent," I replied, giving him the thumbs-up.

"As good as pies on the *Bakur*?"

I nodded my head. "Better."

"How much better?" he inquired.

"The words to describe melt in my mouth with your pie," I replied. He seemed satisfied with that.

"What are you going to do, wash or dry?" Hector asked me.

~~~~~~

At four o'clock that evening the *Styx* was ready for sea duty. Ben started the Cat and we reeled in and secured the steel doors. The water at the stern swirled and turned to foam as we got underway. All hands waved from the *Bakur* as we headed out to sea. I could distinguish Jim by the gleam of his bald head. Their horn blasted a farewell salute and ours blasted back.

The *Vantage*'s stem showed around the point. From the crab pot on the rear top deck, I watched the land fall away.

The wheelhouse doors were open when the surge of the outflushing tide seized us in its mighty grasp. The first visible indication was the increase in our speed. Ben bellowed from the bridge, "We're doing twelve knots!"

We swooped out of the channel, speeding with the swirling eddies and through undertows, past the jagged granite fingers that stretched for our hull. Seals bobbed all about. Seabirds dived and swam in the violence of it all.

"Fourteen knots," I heard Ben say. The jagged points whisked past. "Seventeen! This is the fastest this one ever went."

The *Styx* whizzed out the strait past the bluffs and deep gulches, through cauldrons of whitecaps and swirling eddies, and then over football fields of water stretched so tight it seemed I could walk on it. The lone Inukshuk watched from its post silhouetted against the skyline.

It was the fastest time I ever sped in a ship this size. It was exhilarating, but it didn't last. The digits on the Global Positioning System fell back. Ten miles off the Button Islands, with land shrinking and disappearing astern, we were cruising
~~~~~~

at 8.4 knots. From my perch I counted six green bags of garbage and fifteen bergs. Welcome back to Iceberg Alley. A mile astern, the *Vantage* appeared as if she held a bone in her teeth.

Sunday, September 6

THE EIGHTEEN-HOUR CRUISE TO THE COORDINATES of fleet number one was as pleasant as could be expected under forty-knot northerlies. I wished I had a nickel for every time the windows were awash.

Monday, September 7

NOON ON MONDAY FOUND US in the general vicinity of the fleet, one hundred and sixty nautical miles from Port Burwell harbor. Ben relieved Todd at the helm. It was time to search for buoys.

In the heat of the engine room, I dressed in my dead-of-winter apparel. Don dressed beside me. Jack was over on the starboard side of the engine a few feet from Hector. As I pulled on the layers of clothing, I had a sneaking suspicion that regardless what I wore the cold would creep in. With sweat on my brow I grabbed my woolen gloves, stocking hat, scarf and heavy winter coat and bounded up the steps.

The door leading onto the sheltered deck was open. Before going outside I stopped to button the last buttons and zip the zippers. Outside everything was moving, including the wooden pallet that washed port to starboard in the surges of seawater spewing in through the floodgates. Stainless steel strainers were fitted over each floodgate to prevent fish from washing overboard. Blessing myself, I stepped outside to pull on the last layer, the suit of rubber clothes. The sea did all the talking.

After cautiously climbing up through the open hatch, in the lee of the wheelhouse I stood and looked for buoys. The sea in all directions of the compass was feather white. Steadying myself by pressing my back into one of the deep freezers that were strapped there, I wondered at the technology behind the instruments that enabled us to find a speck of orange in all that surf and foam. A hundred or so lurches later, four of us were huddled together and Ben reduced power. Hector led the way up the ladder to the top of the wheelhouse.

It may have been the same place I had visited before, but it was totally different. The wind almost brought me up standing when I let go of the ladder support and, like a drunken man, staggered forward the ten paces to the exhaust stack. There I held on for dear life and waited for the deck to stop dropping out from under me. Hector, Todd, Jack, Don and Wayne stood forward from me side by side, holding on to different things to stay aboard. It was a gut-wrenching ride even with the ship slowed in.

I couldn't look directly into the wind for very long. Water from my eyes mixed with the water that sprayed from the bow and flowed down my face. The boys who were standing in front of me made a pretty good windbreak, and I soon found myself scanning the quadrant off to port.

After about half an hour, my shivers from fear and apprehension were transformed into shivers from the cold. I could get used to the plunging and lurching, the listing, diving and rolling, and I didn't even mind the seas when they crashed over the bow. But I couldn't adapt to the cold.

Being a slight man, my body doesn't retain heat that well. As a matter of fact, my body doesn't retain heat at all. I don't mind working in the cold. Work generates heat. When I stand around idle the cold tortures me. As soon as my clothes get cold my skeleton rattles and if I mind to let them, my teeth could keep conversation with the pound boards in the hold.

Through my watering eyes I couldn't see anything orange. Both Wayne and Todd held binoculars most of the time. This was the most crucial part of the voyage. We couldn't haul the gear until after the buoys were located. No buoys means no gear; no gear, no turbot. This was how a successful trip was made. You stood, you held on, you looked and you kept on looking and searching until someone shouted, "Over there!" For now, no one did.

To find the buoys Ben searched the area in a grid pattern. He steered the *Styx* north, past the recorded coordinates. With the depth and swift tides of these waters it was not unusual to find that the fleet had drifted far before it settled on bottom. The water here was close to a mile deep.

One mile past the coordinates Ben turned the *Styx* to the west for a distance of a thousand yards or so. There, he altered course to the south and held that bearing for two miles. From there, he steered west again for a thousand yards, at which point he altered course to the south. He would repeat this search pattern until the buoys were spotted. The southward search took about an hour with the wind and seas pushing us along. It seemed to take forever to go north.

After three hours, all standing up top were suffering from the cold. I could see it in their body language—stiffly huddled together, shoulders hunched, eyes peeled for orange. The general consensus was that we should have located the fleet by now. Could the depth sounder be malfunctioning? Maybe the fast tides had tangled the mooring ropes so much that the buoys had sunk. Over the years, much gear has been lost up here.

All about was a soup of gray, white and black. Not a thing was orange. My skeleton had been rattling freely for what felt like eternity when Greg made an appearance on the top deck that plunged and listed forty degrees towards a raging sea eight times every minute, whether you were ready or not.

Greg roughly asserted himself between Hector and Todd by pushing Hector to one side. "Knock it off, Greg!" Hector warned, pushing him away out of the lineup. To save his balance, Greg grabbed onto a guy wire that was stretched taut from the spar to the stem.

Not satisfied with Hector's exhortation, Greg, more roughly this time, forced himself back into the lineup by giving Hector a push that drove him up against Todd. "Give it up, Greg!" Todd exclaimed in a threatening tone of voice.

"Knock it off, Greg! That's twice!" warned Hector. Wayne and Don scanned with the binoculars and seemed unaware of the brewing conflict.

Greg must have been eager to rumble because even after Hector and Todd conceded him standing room, adding to my windbreak, he wouldn't stop fooling around. From my precarious perch with the stack housing firmly in my grasp, I felt in tune with the sea. When the hull lurched to port, my stomach would press firmly against the housing. When the hull lurched to starboard my upper body shifted away from the housing to the full length of my arms. When the bow plunged deep or shot skyward, my knees bent deeply.

Out of the corner of my eye, I spotted a body moving. Todd had given Greg a push at the very same time the hull took a large sea on the port quarter. The *Styx* lurched to starboard and Greg almost went overboard. Freewheeling like a drunkard, he staggered the width of the bridge. If it hadn't been for a guy wire fastened to the spar that he happened to grasp at the last instant, he would have been thrown overboard. Sheer fear masked his face. The hull had a sequence to run and, as if in slow motion, he swung out over the edge with only the toe of his right rubber boot left in contact with the deck.

The hull threw back to port. The spring from the taut stay cable combined with the toss of the deck catapulted Greg back aboard. Before he could stop the forward charge, he slammed into Hector's back. Turning to face him, Hector shook a gloved fist and snarled, "Greg, you're cruisin' for a bruisin'."

"Move out of my way!" Greg snapped. "I'm going down."

Instead of backing down the ladder, Greg decided to take the shortcut. He wrapped his arms and feet around the stay wire from the spar and slid down it to the bow. Unbeknownst to him, that particular swell was number four in the sequence of seven. Greg was about to claim a footing on the wet deck when the hull dived deeply into swell number five.

It seemed to me that it took three or four swells to get the ship moving, to gain enough momentum for the hull to have a tendency to punch through the watery hills rather than ride up them to the crests. This was what happened here and seawater cascaded in over the bow, catching him unprepared. Holding on tightly, we waited to see how the breaking sea served him.

The first thing the sea did was wash away Greg's footing and slam him heavily onto the deck. When the *Styx* lurched to starboard, he was on the broad of his back flailing his arms and legs about in the air. In the blink of an eye, he disappeared in the foam.

Swell six surged up more steeply. The hull dove deeper. Incoming seas swept him across the deck and slammed him against the fish tub.

With mouth wide open and eyes squeezed shut, he hollered something that sounded like a plea before it was drowned out by the breaker. There was nothing we could do but hold on tightly and watch. He was on his own. I wasn't sure if he was aware of surge number seven rearing up menacingly, yards before and above the bow.

Ben, seeing his son's plight played out in front of his eyes, thought he might spare him some misery by slowing in and turning leeward. It may have been the right move. But it didn't help. The peeling water that broke over the bow nearly drowned him. Even the green fish tubs shifted from the impact. By turning the bow, not only did the *Styx* dive deeply, the bow sliced a path up and across the wave's face. Most of this water landed on Greg.

In the violence and clamor of it all, with the spray-drenched wind whisking past my ears and spattering my rubber clothes, I thought I heard him utter the word "God," before he again disappeared in the foam. It seemed to me to take a long time for him to show, and the whole of that time he was under water. The floodgates shed the seawater. Two legs kicked at the air. Greg tried to roll over and failed. There wasn't much life left in him.

Ben rushed out of the wheelhouse and yanked Greg to his feet. It appeared to me that it took a hugh amount of effort just for him to lift his dripping head and glare up at us all looking down.

Ben shouted, "Couldn't any of you help him?"

"There was nothing we could do, Ben!" Wayne snarled back. "He was caught out in a sea and you knows yourself there was nothing we could do. Why didn't he climb down the ladder?"

No one wanted to see Greg hurt, but there was nothing we could do in the face of the unforgiving sea. Ben didn't wait for an answer. Instead, he helped Greg inside and the buoy search continued.

"Cold, Mick?" Jack asked, turning to face me, robbing me of my lee.

I replied, "Yes, you can call me Popsicle Pete. How about yourself?"

"I'm not too bad," he said. Water streaked down his rubber clothes and I could clearly see his naked Adam's apple. My Adam's apple was double wrapped with my scarf. "Yes, you looks cold." He added, "Why don't you go below and clean up the galley? Take your time, you know."

"That's fine by me," I replied, thinking of the heat and warmth I had left behind in the engine room.

"Well, do that now," he said. "We'll be down later on for a cup of tea."

Without further ado, I cautiously climbed down the ladder, taking a last look for a dot of orange in a wild ocean of white, black and gray.

Three o'clock that afternoon, Todd spotted the buoys in the turbulence and everybody was eager to make confirmation. It was the northern end of fleet number one, not even close to the recorded coordinates. The crew made ready to pull the fleet aboard.

Being unfamiliar with this procedure I decided to stand back, stay alert and wait for someone to tell me what to do. After all, I was the extra hand.

Slowly and cautiously, Ben steamed up to the buoys. Keeping them on the starboard side, he was careful not to entangle the mooring rope in the fish or the blades. If that happened and we could not free ourselves, the *Styx* would be rendered helpless in the seas.

Getting the fleet aboard was a team effort. The buoys had tangled about the mooring rope to such an extent that they were almost submerged. The two starboard-side portals on the sheltered deck beside the picking table were opened. Wayne held a noose of rope like a lasso in his hand. When the buoys rubbed along the hull, he leaned out through the portal and tossed the noose.

Todd stood beside him with a gaff (a slender wooden pole with a hook attached at one end), ready to push the noose over the buoy if necessary. Once the buoy was roped, Wayne wrapped the rope around the gurdy and pulled it tight. Using the controls mounted close at hand, the metal wheel, which was about the size of a fifteen-inch car tire, began to turn in a counterclockwise direction. The gurdy's metal teeth seized the rope and the buoys rose from the sea.

Constantly watching the buoys, Wayne skillfully manipulated the main engine controls to keep the *Styx* in position. From now on, his job was the most important of all.

At the same time that Wayne and Todd were roping the buoys, Hector was standing at the ready on the top deck. The high-fly buoy, undetectable by the radar because of sea-clutter, was too long to be taken in through the portal. It had to come in over the rail. When the high-fly rose up on the swell beside the hull, Hector reached out and grabbed and pinned the long wooden handle against the rail. Holding on with all his strength, he paused for the hull to roll back to port.

Below on the shelter deck, using a knife, Wayne cut the rope that tied the high-fly to the other three buoys. When the hull listed to port again, Hector used the momentum to pull the high-fly buoy with the sharp metal reflector plates in over the rail. Walking with it to port, he tied it securely with the others.

On the shelter deck, Todd handed the mooring rope to Hector, who was standing at the stern beside the pounds assembled to hold the gear. From there he started to pull back, carefully coiling the mooring rope on the deck in such a manner that it would not tangle when it was shot out again. Pulling the nets off the bottom was a job shared by two men. On this haul, Hector and Wayne would reel in the mile-long mooring rope, a continuous process that takes approximately ninety minutes. As Hector hauled back, he sang to the noddies that fluttered around us despite our distance from shore and the heavy weather. The birds seemed to know what was on the go. Fleet number one was rising up from the seafloor.

Even with a rusty claw hammer it took me close to half an hour to untangle the buoys. The ropes were tightly twisted up into knots that reminded me of a hangman's nooses. The most prominent sound on the shelter deck above that of water sloshing about my feet came from the gurdy. The immense weight of the fleet put such strain on the mooring rope that it cracked like exploding firecrackers.

Ideally, a fleet is pulled from the northern end. This is much easier because the southward drift of the dragger on the tides helps to pull the nets from the seafloor. To haul a fleet of gear from the south, not only would the gurdy have to pull the immense weight of the fleet and its contents, it would have to pull the ship against the tide as well. That approach often costs a ship gear.

Everyone was ready and waiting when the rock clanged on the picking table. "Nets up!"

Todd untied the knots in a few seconds and Hector secured the line to the stanchion. "You pull from the gurdy, Mick," Wayne said.

"Yes, sir," I replied, moving inside to the picking table next to him. Hector took up position behind me next to the open portal. Todd set up shop across the table. Grabbing both the headrope and footrope together in my hands, I began to pull.

No more than two feet in front of me the wheel spun at about thirty-five rpm. I soon discovered that I had a small window of opportunity in which to do my assigned duty relatively easily. As the wheel turned the net towards me, the webbing easily fell from the wheel and flowed into my moving hands. I soon learned that if I pulled too early, the teeth lost their grip on the webbing and the immense weight caused the net to slip back into the sea. Suddenly, violently, the net might drop a fathom before it caught again in the teeth.

The first time this happened, I thought my fingers, which I had entangled in the webbing, had been ripped from my hands. No one seemed to notice, but I suspected they all knew exactly how it felt and I guessed they were waiting all along for it to happen. Not wanting to miss my timing with the "wheel of fortune," I couldn't spare a glance at the looks on their faces.

When I pulled too late, the net would continue on around the wheel and more often than not, in spite of the repeated, vicious tugs I made, would not come free. I'd call to Wayne, who usually had his head out the portal watching the net as it came up. "Back, Wayne," I'd say. He'd stop the wheel and spin it back, and I'd pluck the ropes free.

The first sea creature that came around into my hands was a turbot that weighed about ten pounds. There was something in its rich color that reminded me of American paper money. My job, Hector informed me, was not just to pull the webbing off the wheel and pile it on the table, but also to spread the webbing apart so as to make it easier for the pickers to pick the webbings clean of product and garbage. Garbage included all species other than number one turbot.

Quite an assortment of specimens from the briny deep came to me entangled in the webbing. Most were alien to me until then, including two species of crab: the rock crab and the much, much larger, red spider crab. Also entangled were strange-looking fish Hector called grenadier, with their scaly skin a shade of wet purple. They ranged from one to maybe twenty pounds and usually came to me with their internal air sacks blown up and protruding from their mouths like balloons.

Chimère, another strange species, came in all sizes, from a few pounds to more than one hundred and thirty pounds. These deep-water fish were black in color with faces that reminded me of a porpoise, sleek bodies and dorsal fins, hardly any eyes and what looked to be a full set of teeth. They were usually dead when they came around to me, and they tangled the webbings up something awful.

The webbing snarled an array of colorful starfish, coral-crusted rocks and some sea cucumbers. Also entangled were sponges that gave off such a foul odor that I was almost sick. All of this was thrown dead, dying or dismembered out through the portals where the noddies fluttered, fought and feasted.

When a turbot approached the wheel entangled in such a way that the immense weight of the fleet would squash it, Wayne used a short-handled gaff to direct the turbot away from the pressure and to my hands in good condition.

The garbage never received the same consideration. Most were subjected to the crushing pressure that squeezed them to pieces before being spun around to me. The chimère burst open in a snow-white flash of solid white meat. The crabs were crushed to pieces. The sharp, spiny pricks pierced both pairs of the gloves I wore and stuck into my hands.

Across from and behind me, Todd and Hector picked the nets clean. Garbage went out the portal, turbot went in the holding tank. When picked clean, Don and Jack pulled the net from the picking table and spread it out about their feet in the starboard pound as they had in the hold. The *Styx* rolled from side to side and pitched from stem to stern constantly. The ropes, squeezed dry by the strain, cracked in front of me.

The net went too far around with the wheel. "Back, Wayne!" The wheel spun back. I plucked too hard. The net was snatched from my fingers. For a while my fingers were numbed and I feared the ropes would break. I found it hard to stand up. To get the power necessary to pull, I had to press my left hip against the edge of the table.

Sometimes, when the ship rolled to port, my upper body swayed in over the picking table too far and the teeth lost their grip. Rip! On other occasions, the ship rolled off to starboard and I lost hip contact with the picking table. Along with contact went my stability, and I'd have to stop pulling in order to grab the edge of the table before I fell into Wayne, who usually had his back to me with his head out the portal watching the net and using the controls to keep the ship in position. By the time the hull tilted back to starboard and my hip struck the table, my time was off again. "Back, Wayne!"

The Fisherman's bend knots may have been easy to untie, but they also caused me much misery. The sheer weight of the fleet and contents squeezed the knots deeply into the teeth and my first pluck never jarred them. With the wheel still turning, hoping not to have to ask Wayne to stop, I viciously plucked a second and a third time.

"Back, Wayne." The wheel spun back a quarter revolution and stopped. Abandoning the controls, Wayne grabbed the ropes and together we plucked the knots free of the teeth. The wheel spun again.

The second and the third nets came aboard and garbage kept the pickers' hands busy. Sometimes the pickers fell behind and the table became heaped with webbing and entangled sea creatures. At those times Wayne would stop the wheel and we'd all pick.

Some of the spider crabs were huge, armed with formidable claws the size of my hand. All went out through the portal in relatively the same way: in pieces. A huge manta ray, big enough to cover a small table, received no pardon from the crush of the pressure.

Sometimes a turbot would fall out of the webbing between the sea and the gurdy. Wayne would spot it right away and yell excitedly, "The gaff, Hector!"

Hector would stop picking and grab a gaff that swung close by. Precariously leaning way out through the portal, he'd hook the sinking turbot, bring it aboard and toss it across the table into the tank. Of the dozens of times Wayne called on him, he never brought in an empty gaff even though the deck plunged and rolled and washed with seawater every six seconds.

Thirty fathoms into the fifteenth net, with the turbot scarce and the garbage picking up, we encountered a rogue swell. Rogue swells roam all oceans and bring the same emotions to mariners as the word growler.

Rogue swells are higher and move faster than the conventional ocean swells. As the rogue overtakes a smaller, slower swell, they combine forces and become a mountain of water, with troughs much deeper than normal. When a rogue swell rises to a greater height than a ship is in overall length, the ship can be tossed stem back over stern; ass over teakettle, more or less.

As fate should have it a gust of wind and the seas combined to spin the hull around one hundred and eighty degrees despite Wayne's best efforts manipulating the controls. As a result the *Styx* took the rogue side on. Wayne saw it coming. "Watch yourself, boys!" he yelled. The gurdy stopped.

At first, I was relieved to be able to get a break. I turned my head to peer out through the portal and saw the sea surging up ominously, turning the shelter deck dark. We rolled into its trough before climbing up the steep lathered face. The net retarded the natural roll of the hull and the mountainous water monster slammed into us. Turning my back to it with my heart in my mouth, I held on to the picking table for dear life.

The force of the deluge struck me in the kidneys, punched the breath out of me and slammed me against the table. Up we rode, up and up, listing off forty degrees. The picking table transformed into a water slide. Teetering on the rogue's back, the hull hesitated for just an instant before free-falling into the trough. Down we plunged and rolled and I guess, because of the plucking action of the hull on the nets, the gurdy made a loud, metallic "snock!" The webbing was ripped from my hands. The gurdy was broken. The fleet had to be reset.

All hands took over immediately. Hector, Todd and I grabbed the webbing in a futile attempt to impede the fleet's plunge to the bottom. Don hastily grabbed the end of the mooring rope and passed it along outside the hull to Wayne's outstretched hands. I held on with all my might while Jack cut the net at the knot and tied fast the end Wayne passed to him; and "fast" it was.

The rock was readied and hastily tied to the footrope. Ben poked his head out the door. "What's going on, boys?"

"The gurdy broke; we got to reset the net!" Wayne yelled at him.

For a big man, he moved like a cat to help us out, and in less than half a dozen rolls and washes everything was made ready and the rock splashed into the sea. The mooring rope whizzed out. Ben went inside to record the coordinates.

We looked at the gurdy. "Sounded like the shaft sheared," Don said, apprehension saturating his voice. "We got to take it apart. Todd, go in and bring up the tools."

Jack tied the buoys to the end of the mooring rope and made ready to throw them over the side. "That sounded serious to me," Wayne said, looking dubiously at the gurdy.

The ship established itself in the rough seas, settling on a course due north.

Before I had time to smoke a cigarette, as Ben watched from the door, Don lifted the shaft from the housing. The side axle was pulled out in two parts, the break shining up at a jagged angle. "Just as I suspected. The shaft is sheared. The gurdy's history," Don confirmed glumly.

"Great start, now, isn't it? We haven't pulled a fleet back yet and the gurdy is gone," Ben said, spitting on deck two or three times. "We don't have a spare one like that aboard, do we, Don?"

"No, sir. There's nothing aboard this one like that," Don replied, shaking his head.

"We'll have to mount the spare one," Wayne suggested.

"Let's get at it, then," Don replied.

Trying to lighten the mood, I said, "I could dart up as far as the auto supply center and pick up a new one."

"I wish," Don said. "I wish."

Replacing the gurdy wasn't an easy task. First we had to take apart the wooden planks that formed pounds about the deck to contain the turbot and garbage that fell off the picking table or dropped from the gurdy. Then, we had to take apart the picking table. We lowered down the spare gurdy from the top deck and hoisted the disabled one up and strapped it to the rail. Wrestling the spare gurdy in place, Don got all our attention when he declared, "It's not high enough."

"What!" exclaimed Wayne. "Too short?"

"Yes, by about three inches," Don replied in a dejected tone, taking a measure with a tape. "We'll have to build a base and raise it up. Todd, go in and bring out the torch, hoses, welder, rods and the grinder. I'm going to need some angle iron. And tell Ben to head her up so the deck don't wash so much. I'm not an underwater welder."

Tuesday, September 8

It was the wee hours of the morning before we were ready to receive turbot again. Not for a single second for the duration of those hours did the *Styx* sit still, and the decks were constantly awash. Welding the gurdy to the deck took the most time. It was a combination of superb seamanship and wizardry on Don's part, but finally the replacement gurdy stood as tall as the old one had. The picking table was reassembled and the tools, torches and materials were all stowed away. Everyone was exhausted.

The weather forecast wasn't good. The thirty-five-knot northerly winds were forecasted to increase overnight and blow fifty to sixty knots. Ben told everyone to get some sleep and we'd begin again at first light. There'd be no stopping then until the weather stopped us.

～～～～～～～～～～～～～～～～～～～～～～～～

The fifteen gill nets we had aboard had entangled approximately twenty thousand pounds of sea creatures. Just four hundred pounds of turbot were iced in the hold.

Ben seemed most perplexed about the turn of events. "The tides up here are so vicious!" he exclaimed as we were having a lunch in the galley before turning in. "I never witnessed the like before! We're going to have to tie on an extra buoy and another hundred fathoms of mooring rope and forget the high-flys, Hector. They only serve to tangle everything up."

Ben informed us that he had been talking to Jerry on the *Vantage* earlier. They were faring no better, maybe worse. Having searched all day, they had found only the southern end of two fleets. While attempting the pull from the south, both fleets had parted. They had searched until dark in the rising seas but had failed to find any other gear. The *Vantage* was headed for Port Burwell to escape the impending storm. The *Styx*, a bigger ship, had no qualms about riding out fifty or sixty knots of wind. We wouldn't be pulling gear; we'd jog it out, head-on into it, at slow speed, just like we were doing now.

～～～～～～～～～～～～～～～～～～～～～～～～

The search for buoys resumed in a cold gray dawn. I held on tightly to the smoke stack and surveyed a quadrant to port. At

8:30 a.m. Ben stormed up atop the wheelhouse beside us. "What's wrong with your eyes, boys?"

"Why?" Todd asked.

"Well, the lot of you must be blind not to see the buoys right there. What are you doing up here, sightseeing?" he added sarcastically, pointing off to port.

Sure enough, there on the water about fifty yards to port glowed the orange bobbers. Nobody answered Ben's question. Instead, in single file, we cautiously climbed down the ladder and prepared to bring the fleet in. Not very deep inside, I knew this was going to be a rough haul. I had witnessed seas more vicious than these, but never had we stopped to haul a fleet of gear.

I stood for a spell in the lee of the bridge, bonding with the deep freezer. Ben opened the starboard door of the wheelhouse and stepped outside to watch the metal reflector plate of the high-fly sway back and forth and scrape along the hull.

Timing was everything to Hector, who stood beside the rail at the ready to pull the high-fly aboard. After he had it securely tied to the railing with the others, he looked at me and said, "Going below? Come down out of the cold."

It was Don and Jack's turn to pull in the mooring. They were the only two bodies on deck when I went down. On the picking table lay a tangled mess of orange buoys and hangman's nooses. "Mick, clear that away, will ya, before you goes in?" Don said, standing at the controls with his hooded head out the portal watching the mooring crack aboard. Frequently, he'd stiffly turn his whole body to check the gurdy and to consult the rudder indicator mounted close at hand. As required, he manipulated the throttle and transmission. The mooring rope cracked to the wheel. So far the gurdy was doing the job.

Jack stood at the stern pulling the mooring rope of fleet number two back from the gurdy. By the time the rock clanged on the picking table, he would be standing on three feet of rope. Forty minutes later I tied the last untangled buoy to the railing. My job was completed.

Jack pulled at a steady rhythm, watching the sea as he worked. "Go in, get warm and have something to eat," he said. "We'll be at it for the next five or six hours straight. How do you like turbot fishin' so far?"

My first reaction was to say that I didn't. But I answered him saying, "I'm like Leonardo da Vinci in the Caramilk commercial on television when, as he was painting the *Mona Lisa*, he was asked if he had solved the mystery as to how the caramel was placed inside the chocolate and he replied, 'I need more time.'"

"You'll have lots of time then," he replied, steadily pulling back. "We got another five or six weeks yet to catch two hundred and fifty thousand pounds to make a good trip of it. So far we've got four hundred," he said with a grin and a toss of his head.

"Go ahead, Jack, make my day," was all I could say.

He laughed and started to sing, "Michael, row the boat ashore." Through the portal the sky appeared dreary and threatening. With the hood of my rubber coat up, I poked my head out and the wind and spray snatched my breath away. At first glance it was hard to distinguish where the sky ended and the sea started. Between the two was a layer of mist and above the mist was a gloom bed of impending weather. Right before my face, almost close enough to touch, noddies wheeled and soared.

"Mona, take a break," I heard Jack say. "If you don't, you'll regret it. Mark my words! You only got forty minutes before you'll be back at it again."

Pulling my water-streaked face inside, I replied, "Yes, I think I will."

The heat was abundant in the engine room and, with relish, I shed my clothes and swung them to warm and dry before heading to the washroom, holding on to something every step of the way.

I didn't have a big urge to eat. Had I a choice between food and sleep, I would have chosen sleep without hesitation. But it was out of the question for the next few hours, so I chose Corn Flakes. Holding on to the half-filled bowl the entire time, I ate my fill.

Hector came out of his room with towel in hand. Pausing before entering the washroom, he said, "Put the kettle on, will you, please?"

"Yes, right away," I replied, rising from the table with the heave of the hull.

"And put down some toast and a dozen eggs to boil," he added, before he closed the door.

The stovetop was railed with tubing to prevent the pots and pans from shifting around. By the time I had the eggs on, Todd came, bleary-eyed, into the galley with a towel and a shaving kit. Holding onto the table he gazed out the porthole and said more to himself through a yawn and a scratch, "There's forty miles of wind on out there now."

Before I could comment, Hector came out of the washroom looking fresh and clean. The toaster popped. "It's a little choppy this morning, Hector," Tod greeted him.

Standing with bowl in hand, I peered through the porthole over the sink to see the same wind chiseling whitecaps on the backs of the receding sea swells. Every six seconds or so, the porthole was completely underwater. It was like being inside a washing machine.

Wayne came out of the room as Todd exited the head. The galley was filling up as we all got ready for the next fleet.

Wayne went in the washroom and closed the door. I buttered the toast.

"Put down a couple slices for me, would you?" Todd asked.

"Coming right up, sir," I replied.

Hector relieved me of the cooking duties. I placed my bowl in the sink with the other dirty dishes and made my way to my dressing area in the engine room.

The last thing I did before I stepped onto the pallet that sloshed back and forth in front of the door was wrap black electrical tape around my sleeves and gloves. Seals were bloody, heavy and grisly; turbot was slubby. To prevent the slub from rotting my clothes too much, I tucked the sleeves of my winter coat into the long sleeves of the orange rubber gloves and taped them about my arm just as Hector had shown me. Placing the roll of tape back on the step for the next man, I blessed myself, then braced myself and stepped outside and into the violence.

Forty, gusting to fifty, knots of wind makes for a lot of upheaval one hundred and sixty miles out in the Labrador Sea during September. Some seamen believe that a sea precedes a storm, and from the looks of the breakers that surrounded me as I reached for my swinging rubber clothes, I figured we were in for a blow.

Just as my hand touched the rubber suit, the hull lunged to port. Water sloshed in through the floodgates and splashed over me. I was drenched. Reaching again for the swinging rubber suit, I discovered why this iron peg was the only one unclaimed on the entire ship. My rubber clothes were dripping wet up the back of the coat and up the pant legs past the knees.

With time to spare before the rock appeared, I viewed my surroundings through the flurry of noddies from the open portal on the starboard side. Don kept his back to me. All his concentration was on the rope that cracked from the sea. The mist line on the horizon had retreated a little and the clouds had changed slightly to a softer, less threatening gray. From the summit of the twenty-foot swells, I could see surf and foam, in frothing formation, charging south at a frenzied pace. The air was saturated with the sounds of water crashing on water, water crashing against steel, iron clanging on steel and ropes cracking.

A noddy soared past and flew straight into the chain that suspended the fish from the stabilizer arm. The bird spun full circle in the air before striking the sea. As it went by me it tried frantically to get airborne flapping only one wing. Other noddies swooped down to investigate. In a few rolls the stricken bird disappeared from view.

Amid the ever-shifting masses of a hundred shades of gray, I saw a plume of spray. It was a whale. Two whales. It's the little things that make your day. Then for some reason an air of dread drafted over me when Hector's words drifted through my head: "They shoot at everything that comes in range of the rails." Remembering the porpoise of my childhood, I decided to say nothing as the crew filed out.

The rock clanged on the picking table. "Nets up!"

For the next six hours we battled the elements to bring the fleet aboard in one piece. The upside was that no one was idle for a minute. The downside was that no one was making much money. It appeared to me that chimère and crabs loved turbot because for every pound that was tossed into the holding tank, at least fifty pounds of "garbage" went dead, dying and dismembered back into the sea. Frequently, the picking table piled high in a tangle of webbing and sea creatures. Wayne would then stop the wheel of misfortune and all hands picked the net clean.

I'd be thankful for the respite, but it wasn't much of a break. Some chimère weighed as much as I did and it was a battle to get them de-webbed and out through the portal. Hector didn't mind it a bit. Deftly, he'd grab an entangled creature off the table and hold it against his chest. Watching it closely, he'd spin and turn it and pull the webbing apart until the creature popped magically into his hands. As he picked, he'd watch me struggle and often offer vital information. He showed me what parts of the bodies to hold on to and what parts to avoid. Some creatures were armed with formidable defenses that could tear a careless or unknowing hand to pieces.

"Pick it, Mick, don't play with it," I heard Jack say from the aft pound as I struggled to free a big, dead specimen from the tangle of monofilament.

Turning towards him, I replied, "Easy for you to say."

"It's not all that easy back here, Mickey boy," he replied, standing with one hand for the ship as he and Don waited for us to clear the webbing. "You can have a spell back here by and by if you like."

"I'll look forward to it," I replied as the sharp quill of a spider crab drove an inch into my sore hand.

Untangling the dead corpse of a giant manta ray, I began to think of the wastefulness and destruction of commercial fishing. Looking at the dead ray, I remembered seeing a television documentary that featured Jacques Cousteau swimming with and filming one just like it. This one would fly the cold currents no more. Clearing it from the last of the meshes, I drove my fingers into its agape mouth and lifted it off the table. Landing belly up in the sea, it did not right itself. I paused for a moment to watch the glowing white belly sink slowly down into the black briny deep. A little piece of me went with it.

About then, Greg made his debut, swaggering up to the holding tank. Without speaking, he drew out a knife and rubbed it rapidly a few times across the honing steel before reaching into the tank for a turbot.

Turbot were scarce, but the few we threw in the holding tank were big—some weighing forty pounds and more. Some turbot were scrubbed white in places where they had been rubbing on the ocean floor. The garbage outweighed the turbot by at least sixty to one. The *Styx* bobbed around like a cork. We worked like wet dogs and the noddies feasted in delight.

Todd went inside and brought out half a bucket of hot water that he tied to the winch. Frequently, he'd dip his hands into the steaming water and let them linger there. I'd become conscious of my own numb hands and I'd concentrate on squeezing them tightly around the cold ropes. One time when the ropes slipped on the wheel, the tips of four fingers on my cotton glove went with it. I suspected it wasn't the first glove that went such a way.

A noddy that had become entangled in the webbing from feasting too close fluttered in over the rail and advanced towards the wheel. Out the corner of my eye, I noticed Wayne stiffly turn to watch the struggling bird. I thought he was going to stop the wheel and set the noddy free. No such thing. Without breaking the flow, the immense pressure caught the frightened seabird and in less than a quarter revolution all life was squeezed out of it. A feather swirled in the wind and stuck fast to Wayne's wet rubber coat. He brushed it away and turned back to watch the net. The noddy went out with the rest of the "garbage."

Hector began to sing the opening verse of "The Gambler." I concentrated on my window, my balance and my footing. The wheel was spinning easier. The ropes cracked less loudly. The net was off the bottom.

The last ten nets of fleet number two produced at least a ton of "garbage" and, as Hector put it, "not enough turbot to fill up my cat's belly."

"We got it here now," Wayne said. The wheel of destruction for a lot of sea creatures stopped spinning.

"What is it?" I asked as a huge tail hung in over the rail entangled in the net. To get a better look I moved to the portal by Hector.

It was a shark, at least ten feet long, and it lay docile in the net. Suddenly, the shark plunged headfirst back into the sea. The wheel began to turn. The shark's tail came around to me. No one seemed sorry when the rock clanged on the table.

Hector began to coil up the mooring rope as Wayne reeled in the buoys. We set to work cleaning up the deck and the catch.

The seas were turning ugly, rising higher, racing faster, as if something to the north had startled them, causing a stampede. Greg was gutting the turbot as was required by the buyers. Head on, gut out.

Todd tossed an empty fish tray on the deck beside Greg. "Throw in some livers," he said.

Without saying a word Greg tossed the turbot livers into the tray. Todd staggered over behind the port winch and pulled down a dip net with an aluminum extension handle. With the dip net held in one hand and liver held in the other, he went to the portal and dropped the liver overboard. The noddies swarmed for the treat. Todd made a sweep with the dip net and pulled it up with three noddies inside. With a wide grin, he set them free about the shelter deck. Five or six dips later it looked like a noddy coop. There were birds everywhere with wings spread, making futile attempts to get airborne.

The sight of them sent my memory back over the years to when I was a small boy of ten spending my summer holidays with my father on a collector boat, the *Clamor*, collecting bulk salt cod from the fishermen of southern Labrador. One hot, sunny evening there was no fish to load. Dad took me for a spin in the speedboat to an island in the bay. The island was a nesting area for a squadron of herring gulls and the young, brown chicks were all about. Dad took two of the young gulls back aboard the ship, and over the next week I grew fond of Gulliver and Gerty. Each morning they'd squawk for me to get up and feed them fresh conners and tomcods. All day long we played hide and seek.

One morning, the young gulls were nowhere to be found. At first I thought they had flown the coop. I went into the galley to ask the cook if he had seen them. Before I entered the galley my nose detected a most repulsive smell. "What's cooking, cookie?" I inquired.

"Gulliver and Gerty," he replied.

Todd removed a frightened noddy from the dip net and cradled it in his arms. Reaching into the tray, he grabbed handful after handful of liver and smeared it into the bird's feathers, not stopping until the bird was completely saturated from head to tail. Satisfied, with noddy in hand, he walked to the portal and tossed it into the wind.

The bird could not fly away. Within an instant after it landed in the foam it was attacked viciously by another noddy. Then another and another. Within a single roll thirty noddies were viciously picking the one that could not fly away. When the feeding frenzy was over, the noddy floated dead on the sea, picked to death.

They weren't finished with the noddies, yet. With a short piece of fishing line in his teeth like a calf roper at the rodeo, Todd caught two birds and held them bottoms up by the legs. Upside down the pair picked viciously at each other. When Todd tossed them out the portal, they both struck the foam at the same time. The last I saw of them they were still picking viciously at each other.

No one said anything. I didn't say anything. I bit deeply into my tongue. Suddenly, I became sick to the pit of my stomach.

Hector began to sing. Without saying a word, I set about catching the frightened birds that flapped about the deck and tossed each and every one into the wind. No one asked me to pass them liver. No one asked me for fishing line. I didn't care what they thought.

~~~~~~

Greg had finished gutting the last turbot when Ben appeared in the doorway and announced that he was setting course for Port Burwell harbor. The forecast called for gale-force winds for the next couple of days. Pulling gear would be impossible. To stay at sea might jeopardize the quality of the little bit of turbot iced in the hold.

"Shoot out the nets we have aboard," Ben ordered. "Join up the fifteen of fleet number one to this fleet and we'll shoot it all out together. Tie on an extra buoy and forget the high-fly. The long pole tangles everything up."

"Yes, sir," Hector replied.

~~~~~~

Within ten minutes the fleet was ready to be shot out again. The *Styx* assumed a northerly course. "Buoys gone," Hector shouted. The mooring rope spewed out. "Rocks gone…Nets gone…Buoys gone." The fleet was bottom bound. Ben entered the coordinates for the Button Islands into the GPS and the swells attacked the starboard side. It was 1:30 p.m. and, from the looks of things, we were in for a long, hard punch.

After dinner when I went on the bridge, Ben was in command, curled up in the chair. The seas seemed intent on toppling us over. The thirty-five hundred pounds of turbot on ice in the hold did nothing to settle the dragger in the turmoil. How many breakers broke in those one hundred and forty nautical miles, no one knows. If only I received a dime for each one, they could keep my share of the turbot.

It was dawning on me that turbot fishing in the Labrador Sea in September was almost on par with sealing in the North Atlantic in March.

~~~~~~

It was pitch black outside when I went on watch at 10 p.m. Pitch black and violent, one hundred and twenty four nautical miles out to sea, plunging headlong at 5.3 knots. The biggest concern was keeping the windows intact and the stabilizers in place. A smashed window caused flooding of the electrical instruments and would leave us helpless. A broken stabilizer arm meant having a ton of metal and chain dangling beneath the hull. I thought of abandoning ship and getting out in the aluminum boat on a night like this to try and fix it. "No thanks," I said aloud. "If this ship goes to the bottom tonight, I'm cuddling a rock in my arms and going directly to Davy Jones's Locker." Sitting there with my heart in my mouth one instant and down by my belly button the next, a noddy ghosted through the sporadically moving spotlight and suddenly, the breakers seemed to crash right through me. Like the *Styx* my spirits dropped. Unlike the *Styx*, they failed to rise. Rock-a-bye sailors on the sea top, when the wind blows the ocean will lop. When the bow breaks, the vessel will fall. Down will go vessel sailors and all.

Wednesday, September 9

I TOOK ALL THE GLOOM AND MORBID THOUGHTS to bed with me. Try as I might I could not shake them off. At four in the morning I relieved Hector at the helm. Before he went below, I spoke to him of the senseless destruction and waste that was disturbing me.
~~~~~~

Hector said, "I know where you're coming from. You do what you feel you must. I got to work here with this crew and I would pull them out of the water. Would you?"

Would I pull one of them out of the sea? Would I risk my life for one of them? The floor tilted to port and a shudder coursed through the hull and the windows foamed white. Pushing off from the chart table I walked the three or four steps up the thirty-degree grade and flung open the top half of the port-side door. A blast of wind greeted me. I hardly felt it.

Propping myself against the bottom half I molded myself to the frame and rolled with the punches. Would I go out in that to save one of them? Water sloshed off the roof and dripped down. The wind chopping around the corner whipped some of it in my face.

"Close the door, Mick, you're freezing me out!" In the chair, Hector sat rubbing his bare arms vigorously. The chart flapped on the table. I closed the door and sat in the rumble seat. Water spattered all the forward windows.

"Yes, Hector, I would pull them from the sea," I said after a while. "I don't think I'd do it because I wanted to. I think I'd do it out of reaction."

"That's good," he said. "I'm sure they'd do the same for you. It's time to call the boys."

"You call them when you go down."

Thursday, September 10

NORTH 60-24-713, WEST 64-49-493. AT 4 P.M. the day was dreary wet. The fifty-knot winds carved whitecaps in Port Burwell harbor. On the bow of the *Styx* the temperature was -4°C when Jim made fast the bowline to the *Bakur*. All the crew of the collector boat were on hand and appeared to be starving for something to do, someone new to talk to. We'd be off-loading our catch right away. The *Vantage* was moored in Mission Harbour. Their twelve hundred pounds of turbot was already in the *Bakur*'s blast freezers and there was plenty of room in there for ours.

After an exchange of greetings, the hatch covers were removed and the boom of the *Styx* was positioned over the hold. I reported to the hold with Hector, Todd, Jack and Don. Wayne wasn't on deck. He was sick in his bunk with his gut filled with Gravol. Ben was aboard the *Bakur* with Captain Kirk. Greg passed down the white fish trays that Todd had stowed haphazardly around a side pound. After the remaining ice was shoveled out of the way into a forward pound, Hector and I worked the starboard pound while Don and Jack worked the port pound. Kneeling in the middle of the iced turbot, Hector and I dug them out and placed them in one of two trays Todd had placed on the floor. Don and Jack did the same on the port side. When these trays were filled, Todd placed two more empty trays on top and we'd fill those. When the trays were piled and filled to a height of five trays, a steel harness was lowered from the boom and hooked to the bottom two trays. Under the watchful eye of the signalman standing above, they were hoisted up. During the hoisting, we hid in a pound out of danger until the boom swung them clear of the hold and onto the *Bakur*. Several times the trays struck the coleman as they were being lifted up or a strap unfastened and the whole load came crashing down. When this happened the turbot weren't damaged, but any of us could have been killed. Several of the plastic trays broke on contact.

It didn't take long to empty the pounds. In an hour the hold was sprayed clean and ready for more. Everyone was concerned about finding the gear for it could be a while before we could get back out to the grounds. All the while the vicious seas and swift currents were twisting up the mooring ropes, possibly enough to sink the buoys.

Finished in the hold, I wanted desperately to get off our ship, so I jumped aboard the *Bakur*. I stood and watched the turbot men work. Two men picked up a tray of turbot and emptied it out into a long stainless steel basin that extended fifteen feet beneath the overhead forecastle housing. Beside the basin, two on each side, four men stood wielding knives. From the basin they'd take the turbot and cut off the tail and the head. The turbot was placed on trays. The reject heads and tails were directed into a chute that emptied into the sea between the two boats.

Jim was one of the knife wielders. He was dressed in rubber boots and clothing. He nodded for me to come over. "What do you think of it all?" he asked.

"How much time do you have?"

"All the time in the world," he replied, decapitating a thirty-pound turbot and tossing the head in a tray that held a whack of them.

"Why are you keeping the heads?" I asked.

"Turbot cheeks," he replied, reaching for another. The two men dumped in another trayful. "Ever eat 'em?" Jim asked, not missing a stroke.

"No," I replied, "I can't say I have. I have heard of them, though."

"Oh, my son, they're some good. I'm cutting out some to bring home. They're just as good as scallops, they are, and just as rich, too."

"Sounds good to me. How do you cut them out?"

"After we're done, I'll show ya. Nothin' to it if ya got a sharp knife."

I walked around the ship then to see what was happening elsewhere. Following the turbot into the forecastle area I found men grading, weighing, wrapping in plastic and packing them in cardboard boxes that were weighed and marked before being stacked in the blast freezers. Kim, the Japanese inspector, oversaw it all. To one side, more than a dozen trays of turbot were ignored. Framed in the wheelhouse window watching it all was Ben.

He was livid when the mate brought up the tally sheet. He stormed out to where Kim was standing with the tally sheet flapping in his hand. "This can't be right!" he blared, stopping beside Kim, roughly shaking the tally sheet in front of him. "We're only credited with twenty-five hundred pounds. What's wrong with that turbot?" he exclaimed, pointing to the ignored trays that lay on the deck.

Kim casually looked from the sheet to the fish trays and with two fingers displayed before Ben's gnarled-up face, he replied, "No good. Number two. We pay only for number one."

"Number two!" Ben bellowed. "What do you mean number two! There's nothing wrong with that turbot!" he said, pointing to the trays. To emphasize his point, he reached down and snatched up a big thirty-five pound specimen. A group of fifteen men watched him do so.

Kim casually inspected the great fish. He pointed at the white marks on the belly. "Scrubbed," he said simply.

"Scrubbed!" Ben blared in mock echo. "Scrubbed!" he repeated, holding up the great fish. "There's not one thing in God's world wrong with that turbot."

"Scrubbed. Number two," replied Kim, sticking to his guns. "We pay only for number one."

Ben threw the turbot over the side and stomped aboard the *Styx*. The men lifted the fifteen trays of rejects and emptied them over the side. More waste.

"Come here now, and I'll show you how it's done," Jim called. Lumbering over, I stood beside him watching as he stuck the pointed tip of his sharp knife in the cheek of the turbot head. With slight up and down sawing movements of the blade, he cut smoothly around the cheek and slowly spun the head around. A quarter-inch from having made a complete circular cut, he stopped and removed the blade. Flipping the "loony-sized" circle of meat out from its lodging, he peeled off the skin. The piece of uncut skin held the strain that was necessary to peel the flesh from the skin. Holding up the treat for me to see, he tossed it into a bag and flipped the head over to cut out the other cheek. "Nothing to it," he said. After the other cheek was in the bag, he threw the head into the reject chute. It splashed in the sea.

"Charlie's knife is there. He won't mind if you cut some."

With knife in hand I selected a turbot head from the tray and began. "The cook is frying a few later on. Come over and have a feed," Jim said.

"Sounds good," I replied. We were practically alone. A couple of the men were working aft, spraying out the fish trays and stacking them forward. Noises came from the forecastle. The smell of cooked supper drifted on the chilly winds and blasts of cold air escaped from the freezers. "Jim, what does Captain Kirk think about killing things?" I inquired.

"What kind of things?"

"Birds, seals and anything else that happens to come within range."

"He wouldn't have it," he replied. "The other day Grant took a shotgun from his room and shot a seagull. The skipper heard the report and rushed out to see what was going on. He saw Grant holding the gun and the dead bird on the water. 'Did you shoot that?' he asked Grant. Grant replied, 'Yes, skipper, I did.' The skipper asked him if he had planned on eating it. He replied that he had not. The skipper told him that someone had better." Jim worked away methodically; the cheeks were piling up.

"What happened?" I asked, putting a scattered cheek in the bag.

"The skipper took the gun from him and told him to report to the bridge with any shells, making it clearly known to everyone that he wasn't going to tolerate any unnecessary killing of any kind. Then he ordered lifeboat drills and we retrieved the gull. I had it for dinner the next day. Why do you ask?"

"Because, nothing alive can come handy to us. What the crew don't shoot, they torture."

"What do you mean, torture?"

"They torture the noddies. I saw it with my own eyes. They captured live noddies with the dip net, smeared them with turbot liver, threw them overboard and watched them get picked to death," I told him.

"What!" he exclaimed, drawing away from me.

"That's not the half of it. They tied two live noddies together and threw them overboard."

Jim seemed repulsed. "Go on! Well, they wouldn't last long aboard this one. They'd be smeared with liver and tossed overboard themselves. Our skipper wouldn't put up with that. Nor would anyone else."

"Ben permits and promotes it. It's a nightmare," I said, glad to have someone to tell.

"It sounds like one," he replied.

"No wonder our luck is so bad. We don't deserve to catch a turbot."

"Well, ye never brought in many, did ye?"

"More than we deserve." The last head splashed into the sea. Jim sprayed the trays clean with seawater. I turned to go back aboard the *Styx*.

"Come over and visit later on," he said as I walked away.

~~~~~~~~~~~~~~~~~~~~~~~~~~~~~~~~

Talk on the bridge of the *Styx* revolved around the tally sheet. Morale was low, disappointment ran rampant. Thus far the
~~~~~~~~~~~~~~~~~~~~~~~~~~~~~~~~

expedition to Ungava wasn't paying out. Among other things, Ben blamed the Japanese. "They can pay us what they like! They own us!" he snarled. "If they decided right now not to buy any more turbot, we'd be out of a job. And not only us, either. That includes the crews on the *Bakur* and *Vantage*, too. There's nothing we can do about it. We're owned in our own land."

No one played the devil's advocate. Don hardly struck a chord.

The disappointment the crew expressed didn't suppress their appetite. I didn't break bread with them, opting instead for a shower. Hymns blared and men chewed when, with a fistful of clean clothes, I passed through the heat of the galley headed for the head. The doom and gloom that shrouded me seemed to wash away with the soapy water. Sometime later, after repeated knocks on the door, I finished up. Fresh and clean, craving nicotine, I made my way to the bridge.

The invigorating feeling continued to build and soon I was quietly singing a song. The fact that I was going to be away from this crew for a while made me sing.

After a few hours of very enjoyable conversation, song, turbot cheeks, tea, pie and cigarettes in the crowded galley of the *Bakur*, Jim invited me to his room. I followed him to the bow, down a flight of wooden stairs to a tiny room smelling strongly of smoke, sweat, feet and farts. A man named Gord was stretched out in the upper bunk on the starboard side. Reg was reclined on the port. Both were smoking. A small table built against the forward bulkhead had seats extended out from the bunks on both sides. A large empty ketchup can placed on the table served as an ashtray. I sat at the table. Jim sat down opposite me.

"Ye never caught much turbot," Reg addressed me without preliminaries.

"No sir, we didn't," I replied, adding, "If we could bring back all we catch, we'd all be millionaires."

"Yes, that's the woeful waste of gillnetting. I was at that for two years and in that time I saw enough destroyed to do me a lifetime. No way in the world can anything last. Nothing in the ocean is safe anymore."

Gord's upper body stretched out of the berth over my shoulder when he tossed a cigarette butt in the tin. "The way I see it is that history is repeating itself," he stated flatly, "and if you like, I'll take the pains to tell you how this is so."

"The floor is yours, my friend," Jim replied.

Gord climbed out of the bunk and sat on the seat beside me. Lighting a fresh cigarette, he said, "The Inuit lived here in Labrador as the Beothuk lived on the island. For thousands of years, they were able to live very well on the resources that were here, and they didn't deplete them.

"We, the white man, came here, were sent here, by the powerful merchants and we worked for them. Because of this we were a different people with a different relationship to the land. The Beothuk only needed to eat; we needed to make money for those merchants in Britain. Because of that we have become disconnected from nature. We were then, and we still are, serving the forces that pay us to take as much as we can from nature with little or no regard to protecting or preserving. In that regard, I think, we have become disconnected from nature."

Gord paused to tap ashes off the cigarette before going on. "Let me give you a recent, prime example: the caplin fishery of Newfoundland. In Newfoundland when I grew up, caplin rolled ashore on the beaches each spring to spawn and, like the Beothuk, we took what we wanted. Some of the caplin we used as food, frying them fresh in a hot pan with butter. Caplin were salted and dried in the sun and eaten that way, too. A great many were smoked. Wagon-loads of caplin were used on the gardens as fertilizer. But lots were left to follow nature's course. Then the world market opened up and there came a demand for caplin that was like a Klondike gold rush. So what happened then was we lost another integral part of the living world because it had become commercialized. And we needed the work so we took part in it."

No one interjected while Gord sat still and silent to collect his thoughts. "So," he continued, "Newfoundlanders, although they are close to nature, are in a paradoxical situation. We only come close to nature to take from it and capitalize from it. Nature is there to serve us and to profit from. This has contributed to the unfortunate conditions we got ourselves into and that is why we are where we are now. As far as I'm concerned, it's not just a local problem. It's a worldwide problem.

"With the collapse of our fishery, the writing was on the wall. The powers that be knew what was happening. It's not something new. I was listening to the fisheries broadcast not long ago when an author of a book dealing with the demise of the cod fishery and herring stocks in Europe was on. This was before the moratorium on ground fish in Canadian waters off the east coast. The authorities knew what had happened over there and they knew what was going to happen here. Just like the Beothuk. *They* knew what was going to happen. Economic forces killed them all.

"So it seems to me that as a people we are like a leaf in the wind with no control of our destiny. Like it or lump it, we are in the same unfortunate position as the Beothuk, and you can mark my words, we will be displaced just like they were. We *are* being displaced. But we were a part of our own demise. We made the rods for our own arses with a lack of any thought for the resource beyond making a living.

"When new fishing practices came along like monofilament gill nets, we quickly adopted these new fishing techniques and, sad to say, they are here to stay. Not so long ago a fisherman asked me if I knew where he could buy some gill nets. He was from the south coast of Newfoundland. I asked him what he was doing setting gill nets on the south coast because as far as I knew, the south coast of Newfoundland was gill net-free for all of history. 'Oh, DFO is going to let us set gill nets now. We never used 'em before, but they're going out now,' he said."

Gord turned to me and said, "Right now, Mick, they won't let us catch a cod for the dinner table, but they'll permit the setting of gill nets in waters that have never seen a gill net before. As destructive as gill nets are they permit more and more of the trash to be set. They are even opening up new areas to gillnetting. That's what the great managers are doing, the same ones that got us in this goddamn mess because they got their goddamn fingers on every aspect of it. For Jesus' sake, you can't piss over the side now without a permit."

Nobody laughed, no one spoke and no one took the floor from Gord. "I can't believe it. They are smart enough for everything else; think they'd develop a biodegradable, environmentally friendly net that breaks down after a period of time. No, no, they won't.

"It takes unfortunate incidents like the demise of the cod and the caplin to be a catalyst for change, although as far as I'm concerned change is coming slower than the Second Coming of Christ."

There were amens all around.

"It all came down to how much the cod was worth. It was like gold, in some ways. We were the miners of that gold and we mined it all away and now all we're left with is the shaft. It sounds like a familiar story, doesn't it? It's the same old story over and over again."

Gord spoke with conviction in a clear and collected voice that changed in tone, pitch and intensity to fill the tiny room, and sent Jim and I reaching for a cigarette. He squirmed and said with a sigh, "I don't know if there are any answers to it. I will assume some responsibility for my inactivity. While people go out and slaughter, I sit idly by and do nothing. If you watch a holocaust of, I don't care what it is, and if you do nothing, well, you're just as responsible as the causers of that holocaust. That is the form of guilt that I carry. There are cruel and callous people in all parts of the world. It's as plain as the nose on your face. Once the fishery collapsed in Newfoundland, the Spanish and the Portuguese, to name two, had to suspend their fishing fleets. What did they do? They went to the poorer ocean-bordering countries like Morocco and made deals with the governments there to catch 'quotas.' The fleets come and wipe out all the fish stocks and all the little boats are tied up on shore and the people get displaced. Doesn't that sound all too familiar? It's Newfoundland over there. Then we have countries who rape and destroy our fish stocks and our habitat who never traditionally fished here. Look, we fought the Japanese in the last war. They've always raped the Pacific. Now they are fishing for squid off Newfoundland while the market is soft. Now, if there's anything soft it's Newfoundlanders' heads!"

The way that Gord's voice rose in crescendo, became filled with frustration, anger and disappointment, the way that his body shifted around beside me and the loud noise when he struck the table to accentuate the point, snuffed out my intent to laugh to lighten the mood. No one else laughed. Jim stared at the ashtray. Reg stared at the ceiling. I stared at Gord. Gord wrung his hands and continued in a lower, more controlled tone. "So, I am, we are, Beothuks, you see. I know enough about what happened to the Beothuks to be able to say that I'm in the same goddamn, doomed boat! The same Jesus spot and going down the same way. Sunk by the same commercial interests, only larger and larger and larger. Now, I'm not allowed to catch a fish to eat for my dinner. And I feel like I want to protest. I want to go get a codfish, walk into the DFO office and slap someone in the face with it. More than likely I'd end up in jail, but maybe that's my destiny."

Gord lit another cigarette and offered a round. We all lit up. The room became like the inside of a smokehouse. Sporadic coughing broke out. Waves broke along by the bow. Gord turned towards me and said, "I'm not an economist. But I know that when I was a kid I could walk on caplin spawn in Sleepy Cove, Twillingate, the beach so covered with caplin eggs that I thought it was gray sand. I walked on it and I thought, 'My, this sand is awful spongy, awful weird.' I reached down and drove my hands almost to the elbows in the sand and scooped some up. And I realized it was billions and billions of caplin eggs.

"Now, we don't see that today because caplin are caught on the open ocean before they get a chance to spawn. The big guys, with state-of-the-art superships equipped with cutting edge technology, scoop them all up. The salmon and the cod went the same way. And now I'm not allowed to catch one for my dinner. That's the part that hurts me the most. Now is that right or wrong?" Gord inquired.

Friday, September 11

MIDNIGHT FOUND ME ALONE ON THE BRIDGE of the *Styx*, thinking about what Gord had said and having a look around. We remained tied fast to the *Bakur* and, all considered, things were pretty civil in Port Burwell harbor. It felt like mid-November. All was quiet down below and above. Other than lights shining in from the *Bakur*, everything was black. After rolling out my bag, I peeled off only one layer and crawled in.

After breakfast, the *Bakur*'s crew loaded sufficient ice to keep cold eighty thousand pounds of turbot. Todd topped up the onboard water tanks, while Don filled the *Styx*'s fuel tanks. Then we slipped the lines and moored up in the harbor. The snow had melted from the hills. The rain-specked wind had increased and veered to the west. Todd came out of the room, and the image of his fishing rod hung from the ceiling of the shelter deck beside the dip net came to my mind. I asked if I could use it.

"Yes," he replied. "Go ahead. There's lures in the tackle box."

"Thanks a lot. I'll put it back. If anyone calls for me, tell them I'm gone fishing."

On the port side, in the area used to stow the moorings, I found some lee to fish. The whitecaps swallowed the expensive lure and I let it sink for fishing's sake. It was then that I noticed the polar bear standing near the shore about one hundred yards away. With head held high he sniffed the wind, undoubtedly drawn by the smell of turbot emanating from the *Styx*. As if he owned the place, he dove headfirst into the sea and began to swim towards me with his nose in the air.

Snick, snick, snick. Greg was trying his eye and I suspected what he was firing at. The bear must have sensed something, too, for it abruptly turned and dived out of sight. After what seemed like a long time, the bear appeared thirty yards from shore. Shortly afterwards, he surged out of the sea on the run. Without stopping to shake off the water, the bear galloped up the beach and disappeared behind the rise with the rifle snicking bullets at his heels. I jigged a few times with the rod and watched the place where I had last spotted the bear. "Nothing alive can come handy to us."

As I fished, a huge fog bank rolled in from Hudson Bay, shrouding the headlands and valleys in a cloak of dampness. Shivering, I reeled in the heavy lure, suspecting that somewhere not far away a great polar bear lay licking its wounds.

In the galley, gospel singers greeted me dressed in their finest Sunday-go-to-meeting clothes, standing around a man playing a piano and singing, "May the Circle Be Unbroken." Wayne watched the TV intently. Jack and Greg sat at the table watching Don and Hector play checkers. I hummed along and poured myself a hot cup of tea.

"Catch anything?" Jack asked.

"I never got a bite," I replied.

"What were you fishing for?"

"I went fishing for fishing's sake."

"And caught nothing?"

"Nothing you could sink your teeth into, if you know what I mean."

"I'm a fisherman," Jack replied. "I know exactly what you mean."

Hector skunked Don before he had a chance to make a king. Greg wanted to play. Both arranged the checkers on the squares.

"When are you calling home?" Don asked Jack.

"I don't know for sure, maybe tonight. Are you calling home?"

"I was thinking about it. We'll give it a try later on," Don replied.

"I'll call, too," added Todd. "Are you calling home, Mick?"

"I don't think so," I replied.

Greg lost the match miserably, and it showed. Armed with three kings, Hector cornered and conquered. Greg was a sore loser and it showed.

"Can't take a beatin', eh?" Hector chided him.

Greg said, "Shift out, Jack," and went into the room and closed the door firmly. Todd wanted to play next.

The checkerboard was a sturdy one made so that it folded together on a hinge to form a box to hold the checkers. One of the crewmen of the *Bakur* had forgotten to take it with him, so it looked like we were going to have it for at least one trip. No one talked much. I ignored the revival meeting and concentrated on the game. Todd was putting up a fight.

The forecast called for diminishing winds over the next few days so it looked like we'd be heading for the fishing grounds in the evening. Everyone was eager to get out and find the gear before the tides twisted up the buoys and the seas swallowed them. We'd be sailing around five that afternoon so as to shoot out the strait in daylight. The *Vantage*, too, was heading for the fishing grounds at that time. I finished my tea as Hector jumped Todd's last king. I shifted out from the table, washed up my mug at the sink and peered out the open porthole at the fog.

As Todd and I cleaned up the galley after supper I watched the rocky crags and jagged points of Killiniq Island whisk by. We were headed back out to sea. The fog had lifted somewhat and only the tops of the headlands were hidden. Gulls and terns flew by; some looked in to see me looking out at them. Seal heads poked through the swiftly moving waters of the strait.

The Button Islands were five nautical miles astern when I brought the garbage to my fishing spot and tossed it over the side. The *Vantage*, with stabilizer arms extended, kept pace with us. The wind was dropping out in Iceberg Alley. The sky was clogged with fog that limited vision to about two miles. A mile to starboard, barely visible in the fog, loomed a five-hundred-thousand-ton iceberg. It claimed a fog bank all its own and just sat there unmoving, oblivious to the seas that crashed against it.

The sea had a soothing effect on me. It always did. Leaning over the rail the foam passed, at times almost close enough for me to reach out and touch it, and when we were deep in a trough it surrounded me completely. The continuous, steady drone of the main engine blended in perfectly with the sounds of the water washing along the hull. The stabilizer arm extended out from our hull and the fish chain, where it entered the sea, formed a continuous string of bubbles. I glanced back at the berg. As big as it was, the fog had swallowed it whole.

Saturday, September 12

ONE A.M. FOUND TODD AND ME ON WATCH. We were experiencing a good time along—on course at a steady 8.7 knots. The sea was calming down, the swells settling back so that the windows received a washing only every thirty seconds. Fifteen bergs and the *Vantage* blipped on the radar screen, all safely away from us. Todd slouched in the commander's chair. I stood at the chart table peering for growlers in the searchbeam. For a while Todd did more yawning than watching, and frequently he'd lift a leg and fart, stinking up the wheelhouse. Craving a breath of fresh air, I flung open the top half of the port-side door.

The draft that invaded the bridge brought water to my eyes. In my peripheral vision I saw Todd shift in the chair. The hull tilted to port and the sea rushed up to greet me. In a very gentle motion it crested and was gone under the hull. Looking up I couldn't see a single star.

"Close the door, Mick," Todd called across the way.

Turning my head towards him, I asked, "What for?"

"I'm freezing to death," he replied, vigorously rubbing his arms.

"What?"

"Close the door, boy. You're freezing the place out."

"What, are you cold?"

"Yes, I'm froze. Close the door."

"What?" I asked again.

"The door! Close the door!" he almost yelled.

Leaving the door wide open I walked up the grade, across the bridge and stopped a foot from him. "I'll make a deal with you, Todd. You quit rotting the wheelhouse and I'll close the door."

"Deal," he replied.

"Deal," I said, turning away to close the door.

We saw no growlers and as the bridge warmed up, I lightened up. "I'm going below for an orange. Want something brought up?" I asked.

"Yes," he replied, turning away from the spinning clear viewer to look at me. "Go in the room and in the drawer under my bunk get a bag of chips and a drink. Take a drink for yourself, if you want it."

At 3 a.m. when Todd and I passed control over to Wayne and Don, the minute pencil dot on the chart was eighty-two nautical miles from the Button Islands, with a relatively clear radar screen.

On the bench, I stripped off most of my clothes and crawled in the sleeping bag. The seas that caressed the port bow were favorable to me and it wasn't long before I was rocked into a deep sleep.

At midday we were in the vicinity of a fleet of gear and most of the crew watched for buoys from atop the wheelhouse. Seas were moderate. The fog lifted. To the west Don spotted a snow-white bird, a ptarmigan, fluttering towards us as if looking for a place to rest. When the bird had fluttered within yards of the rail, Todd put an imaginary gun to his shoulders and aimed at the bird. "Boom! Boom!" he bellowed. The ptarmigan suddenly veered away and headed where there was nothing but sea for more than a thousand miles.

"Boom! Boom!" Hector echoed Todd as the bird flew off. Turning to Todd, he said, "Boom-Boom. That's what we'll call you from now on. Boom-Boom."

Todd didn't say very much after that. He just held on and looked for buoys like the rest of us.

It was three o'clock before Wayne pointed to port and shouted, "Over there!" I interpreted the confirmation received from Todd and Don as my cue to get the hell out of the cold, and I did so without delay. Ben carefully approached the buoys that barely floated on the surface. I untangled the twists and nooses while Todd and Greg brought up the net. Everyone else disappeared inside.

At 11 p.m. the fleet was aboard. Iced in the hold were five thousand pounds of turbot, mostly large but not all number one. We dumped at least fifteen hundred pounds over the side along with what I estimated to be at least twelve tons of garbage, including six sharks. Some starfish may have survived. Many nets were ripped to pieces; often fathoms and fathoms of rope curled around the spinning wheel to be followed only by a huge tangle of webbing. The deck was awash nearly every roll the hull made. Morale was low.

As I was battling to untangle a monster spider crab from the webbing, I said, "Hector, these crabs must be good to eat. Have you ever cooked any?"

"Mick, they are delicious," Hector replied. Both his hands were active wrestling a gut-busted one-hundred-pound chimère from the tangle of webbing. "Once you gets a taste of spider crab, you won't want to throw another one away."

"Well, toss a few to one side, would you? I want a boil later on."

"Will do," he said. Strain showed on his face when he lifted the big fish off the table and grunted it up and out through the portal atop the birds. "I hope we never see another lousy one," he added.

A hooded seal became a fatality shortly after Wayne noticed great bites taken from some turbot bellies. At first we didn't know what was up until Wayne got everyone's attention when he shouted, "Look there!"

The word seal strikes a raw nerve in many fishermen simply because they eat fish. Seals compete with man and should be shot on the spot is the feeling. It seemed to me that once again, in this case, man had been hoisted with his own petard.

Not so long ago, any seal that shoved up its head in coastal waters would be shot. Today, because of federal regulations, no one is permitted to shoot them other than during each spring season. Because the seals are protected, the herd has increased dramatically, to the point where an increasing number stay around the bays well into summer instead of traveling north on their normal migration path. These seals frequent the mouths of salmon rivers and destroy vast numbers of the salmon that return to the rivers each summer to spawn. Of late, there have even been reports of seals miles inland wreaking havoc on the fish stocks. No one is allowed to shoot them, and with the decline of whales and polar bears, they don't have enough natural predators.

This hooded seal was swimming in the swells about fifty yards from the hull with a large turbot in his jaws. Rising up out of the sea, his head whipped viciously from side to side. The turbot flew through the air and landed with a splash twenty feet away. The hooded seal dived again and shortly afterwards broke the surface again with the great fish in his jaws.

"Ben! Ben!" Wayne shouted at the galley.

Two rolls later Ben poked his head out the door. "What?"

"There's a hooded seal out there eating our turbot."

"Where?" he asked, looking about.

"There," Wayne answered, pointing.

"I've got something for him to eat," Ben said before disappearing inside.

A few minutes later Ben stood in the doorway holding a 243 caliber rifle. "This'll fix him."

I was getting used to the gurdy, and although I thought it was the worst job, I could now apply ample strain on the ropes to keep it from slipping and still sometimes be able to glance around. The wheel stopped. We were going to watch Ben take a shot.

One shot was all it took. I figured the seal was just getting his meal, like everyone else.

I didn't pull the whole fleet. Todd pulled in the last ten nets. He complained of cold hands and figured a spell on the gurdy might warm them up. He had been gurdy man before I came aboard and would revert back to gurdy man after I left. "Here comes the Hurdy-Gurdy Man," I sang as I handed over the ropes. I began to pick.

If pulling from the gurdy was rough on the shoulders and hips, picking the nets played havoc with the hands. Hector freed the garbage deftly. Often I'd pass along to him a still partially wrapped crab or chimère that I had lost patience with. "It's all in the wrists," he'd claim as he untangled the webbing. Sometimes he sang, seemingly immune to the stabs of pain that I knew were shooting in his hands. At one time he looked at me and declared, "I loves pickin'."

No one was pleased with the productivity. It was suggested that we needed eighty thousand pounds of number one turbot to remain in contention for the possibility of earning the projected twelve-to-fifteen-thousand-dollar payout. The suggestion that the payout most likely would be twelve to fifteen hundred dollars surfaced. Some of the nets were ripped up so badly that they were really out of fishing order, but they were destined to be shot away again, as they were.

Sunday, September 13

CIVIL SEAS AND LIGHT SOUTHERLY WINDS prompted Ben to shut down the main engine at midnight, 152 nautical miles off Cape Chidley. Under a nonthreatening starless sky the *Styx* drifted south at 1.8 knots. In the bag on the bench, I couldn't warm up. My feet bothered me the most. Rub them as I might the blood refused to flow through veins shrunken with cold from standing for hours on a deck awash with frigid seawater. Pushing back the sleeping bag, I found my woolen socks and pulled them on. Four-thirty a.m. came early.

~~~~~~

At 8 a.m. Wayne roped one of the three buoys that were all but sunk. He and Greg brought up the mooring. I untangled the buoys. The sun didn't shine. The light southerly winds carved cat paws on the ten-foot swells.

As feared, this fleet fared no better than the fleet now in the pound. We feared that quite a bit of the turbot Hector iced in the hold was destined for the bottom of Port Burwell harbor. Plentiful was the garbage, plentiful and big. My estimate was that for every pound of turbot that we threw in the tank, we dumped fifty pounds of dead, dying and dismembered fish, shellfish and birds back into the sea. It was backbreaking, demoralizing work. The final tally was three dips: fifteen hundred pounds of turbot. No one was pleased. It was all Hector could do to sing a few mournful verses. We were not going to see anything close to fifteen thousand dollars. As we picked, I waltzed for a full five minutes with a lifeless chimère that weighed more than I did. Its skin had burst open to expose snow-white flesh and its ruptured guts exposed its breakfast.

"Certainly God, that flesh must be good to eat," I complained. "It must be worth something to somebody!"
~~~~~~

"Not to us," Hector replied. "Besides, if it was, someone would have been here long before now and we wouldn't be catching any."

"You're not much out on that, Hector," I grunted as, finally freed from the webbing, I laboriously lifted the great squashed fish up and out the portal.

The manta rays went out the same way. All too often, I'd suspend one by the tail out the portal and drop it among the noddies, hoping that it might swim away. No way. Time and time and time again the tide flipped them over to show white bellies as they slowly sank into the black. Hour after hour after hour was enough to break the hardest heart.

∿∿∿∿∿∿∿∿∿∿∿∿∿∿∿∿∿∿∿

At 2 p.m. the fleet was fishing again and Ben headed for the next one. It took two hours to discover it one and a half miles southeast of the recorded coordinates. Without delay the mooring was pulled in. While I battled with the snags and snarls, I noticed a plume of spray off to starboard. An instant later I saw another. Two whales were approaching. Before I had the buoys tied in place, both whales were right alongside, maybe lured to the ship by the sounds the gurdy made. I was drawn to the portal to watch them.

They were immense and glorious, at least sixty feet long. They stopped and rested mere yards away. The swells washed over their great broad backs that showed above the water like a capsized ship, almost as long as the *Styx*.

"Ben! Ben!" Wayne shouted at the open door.

Ben appeared in the doorway. "What?"

"There's two whales right alongside," Wayne stated in a hushed tone as if he might drive them away. As Ben turned to go inside, Wayne called after him, "Give it to him in the head, Ben! Give it to him in the head."

One of the whales seemed to be asleep a mere forty yards from me. Slowly it sank in the swells, but the darker form was visible just beneath the surface. I became aware of Todd standing beside me watching. Wayne stopped the gurdy. Show time.

A sea broke over the whale as it lay at peace beside us. As its broad back rose above the wave, just before the sound of bellowing air and flying spray was to reach my ears, the rifle fired. The sharp report startled me and it killed all sounds from the whale. The bullet caused a reaction in the whale that startled me. Instead of blowing spray, it dived sharply. Before disappearing in a direct death dive for the deep, its whole body straightened out like a pencil. Then both whales were gone.

I'm not sure if Wayne shouted praises to Ben or not. All that reverberated inside my shocked skull was the sound of the rifle. Turning towards Wayne I shouted venomously at his back in a clear and harsh snarl: "Jesus Christ, boys! You're not shooting whales! For God's sake, that could have been your dead grandfather out to see how we're doing! No wonder our luck is so bad; nothing alive can come handy to us!" I finished the statement with a kick to the picking table that rattled the stainless steel all the way to the gurdy.

Wayne turned towards me with a shocked look on his face as if to say, "You got a nerve swearing on this boat."

All I wanted was to get this lousy trip over with, to get the hell out of this. I didn't care if I ever saw another goddamn turbot. Come on wind! Come on seas! Come on dark! Come on daylight! Come on October! "Back, Wayne!" I snarled.

The subsequent labor reduced some of my fury; my sore shoulders absorbed some of my spite. Comments were made among the others about the sad state of the nets, the abundance of lousy garbage, the flaming crabs and the scarcity of turbot. I made no comment. I pulled and pulled, watching to see what would be crushed to pieces next. Finally, the rock clanged on the table. "Nets up!"

Todd untied the rock. Hector took the end of the mooring rope, walked astern to the top of the pile of rope and started to pull back. Greg made ready to leave after Todd sprayed him down with water blasting from the hose he used to wash away the pieces of garbage and slub. I began to toss the dead specimens that washed about the deck out through the portal. Beneath the picking table, a fish tray was filled with large red crabs.

"Pass out the cooking pot when you goes in, Greg," Hector said.

"Why?"

"Cause I'm going to give Mick his first taste of spider crab. What do you say, Mick?"

"Sounds good to me, Hector," I replied.

"You're not going to cook that up tonight!" he replied.

"Well, you don't have to eat it if you don't want any. We'll eat 'em." Without saying anything else, he went inside in the warm.

Wayne left the deck. Jack took over the controls. Reaching down I carefully lifted a ten-pound crab with both hands and placed it on the picking table. It spread close to three feet. The body was about the size of a dinner plate, spiked with red needles two inches long. The legs sported shorter tines closer together. On the end of the crushing arm was a formidable-looking claw about the size of my fist. This one had almost escaped the pressure of the wheel. I flipped the spider crab onto its back and ripped the sections of legs from its body. The pot clanged on the table beside me.

The pot held four crabs. The rest I dumped over the side. There wasn't any life in the tray. Todd was cleaning up the deck. Don shed his rubber clothes and, with the pot in hand, he went inside. There were a few turbot left in the tank, so I grabbed the knife and started to gut them. I knew some of them were destined for the bottom of the harbor.

Hector shouted, "Make sure you get all the liver out, Mick."

When I went inside the galley table was dressed in a double layer of paper towels and a can of Pepsi stood at attention beside each paper plate. The crabs were delicious, succulent and juicy with just the right amount of salt. The shell was soft, and instead of sticking into my hands, the needles were spongy and pliable. The joints cracked apart easily to reveal long steaming strands of solid white meat. Water dripped from our chins, sweat appeared on our brows and we all became more cramped. Soon only a few of the smaller legs were left.

"Hector, how come no one has been here and caught up all these spider crabs? To my taste buds they're just as good, if not better, than snow crab."

"They won't pot," he replied simply.

"What do you mean by that?" I asked.

"The crabs won't crawl in a crab pot. I'm not sure why that is. Maybe they are smarter than the average crabs. The only way to catch them is in nets."

Ben was in the chair when I went to my room after the feast. Even though the lights glared he hardly noticed me stripping off and crawling into my bag. He was listening intently to the radio. Jerry was telling him about their day.

"We're not doing much with it, boy. We can hardly find any of the gear and what we do find usually breaks before we get it aboard. What we do get aboard is full of garbage. I'm not sure if it was a good decision to come up here or not. We've been all day searching for, pulling and picking one fleet. What turbot we did catch is small. Oh, the lousy crabs. Aren't they numerous? Over."

"*Styx*, back. Yes, boy, read you loud and clear. Demoralizing it is. But we're up here and we got to give it our best shot. What are your plans? Over."

"*Vantage*, back. Yes, boy, you're right, boy. Hell of a way to make a living, isn't it? I never saw fishing as bad as this before. As for our plans, we're going to get the forecast and see what's coming. I'll get back to you. Over."

"Back. Roger, Jerry. I'll talk to you later on. *Styx* clear."

"*Vantage* clear. Standing by on 2142."

I gave him no indication that I was awake when he hung up the mike and clicked the channels on the radio. I didn't want to talk to him.

<hr>

A voice over the set said loud and clear, "Security. Security. Security. All stations. All stations. All stations. Iqaluit Coast Guard Radio reporting the marine weather forecast. For Cape Chidley and the Labrador Sea, gale-force northerlies forty-five knots gusting to sixty knots. Shifting to gale-force northeasterly in the evening. Temperature high, 4°C…"

As soon as I heard the word "security," which meant, "find shelter," I knew my demands for weather had been heard. I didn't care, lying there. I figured I felt lower than a turbot's belly at the bottom of the Mariana Trench. I wondered if the whale Ben shot had struck bottom yet.

"*Vantage, Vantage, Vantage. Styx*, copy Jerry?"

"Roger. 2182, Ben."

I listened to them talking. Jerry was afraid of the storm. He was heading for Port Burwell with his twelve hundred pounds. He wasn't happy with the way things were turning out, threatening to pull up the gear and head south. Ben said that Ungava Bay, a mere fifty miles from Port Burwell harbor, might be more lucrative. It had never been fished before. There the weather would also be more civil. In any case, we'd be staying out and would pull a fleet at first light or as soon as we found it. If the weather held, we'd pull the fleet of thirty-five that we had to reset when the gurdy broke. After that we'd be heading to Port Burwell harbor.

Monday, September 14

AT 7:30 A.M., UNDER THE PREMISE OF A GOOD DAY to be turbot fishing in the Labrador Sea, the mooring was cracking in. When the rock clanged on the picking table at 3 p.m., the fifty nets yielded sixteen hundred pounds of turbot. With another fleet aboard, that amount had increased to forty-six hundred pounds. Fleet number three parted the lines when we had only ten nets pulled aboard. The rocking of the ship was too much for the ropes to stand. While pulling another fleet, the ropes again parted and another forty were lost. Wayne blamed it on the rough bottom. Given the gaping holes that were in a great many of the nets, he was right on the money.

Tuesday, September 15

THE SEA NUDGED ME AWAKE WITH THE GLOOM of dawn. Ben came up and turned the ignition key to the main engine. The Cat didn't make a sound. With a loud "tut," in a near frantic tone, he said, "What's wrong with this, now!" I rolled back the sleeping bag and sat up. "Mick, go down and tell Don the flamin' engine won't start," Ben ordered.

Don found the trouble to be in the starter. He had to use a screwdriver to get the engine running again. This time we practically steamed right up to the gear, locating it one mile southwest of the coordinates after searching for no more than thirty minutes. The coming storm was north of us where the smoky clouds twirled up like cinnamon rolls and hung threateningly on the horizon. "Come on, let's get it aboard!" Ben exclaimed.

Six hours of relentless pulling and hauling, stopping and going, rocking and rolling, picking and discarding produced five thousand pounds of turbot, not all of it number one. We dumped fifty times more garbage back into the sea than turbot Hector iced in the hold. These nets had been fishing long enough that they should have been full. Many of the nets were riddled with gaping holes. The noddies feasted and the ship rolled continuously, the rising swells spewing through the floodgates more and more frequently as the Fisherman's bends passed slowly around the wheel. Morale was ebbing. None of the crew laughed much. It didn't matter to me anymore.

Wednesday, September 16

AROUND MIDNIGHT THE WINDS STARTED to freshen and the seas increased to twenty feet, surging southward with increasing animosity. From atop the bridge at 2 p.m. Wayne spotted the buoys of the fleet of thirty-five nets in the turbulence.

That was my cue to get down out of the cold. I let the tangle of the buoys wait for half an hour while I sat beside the Cat. After the heat revived me, I shed my rubber clothes and boots. My boots didn't have liners and my feet were numb. As I tried to rub some life back into them, I knew it had been a big mistake not to bring new ones. In the rush to get ready for this voyage I hadn't given much thought to what the weather was like north of the sixtieth parallel.

Number one turbot was scarce. Much to our sorrow, number two turbot was less scarce. Garbage was abundant and holes in the gear plentiful. Conversation was almost nonexistent. The hull lurched a lot and the ropes cracked to the wheel.

Ideally, the net hung from the gurdy straight into the sea. Conditions were far from ideal. Gusts of winds, five-knot tides and the sixteen-foot waves sometimes combined to spin the ship around, exposing us to the brunt of the storm. Wayne struggled with the controls, kicking the Cat ahead, cutting the rudder hard over, gunning the engine astern. The nets were hopelessly tangled in the fish. Ben ordered it taken in. It got worse after that. The noddies alone seemed happy, doing their usual amount of feasting beside the hull.

As bad as it was, as long as it took the nets to come aboard, as much as the elements lashed us, I found some degree of consolation in the fact that turbot fishing was still better than sealing. I recalled being down in the hold of the *Vantage* just a few months ago, waiting for the revolting carcasses to stop raining down so that I could stow them in the pound. Sweat was running freely down my face and shoulders, blood and blubber was on my hands, on my face, in my hair and in my mouth. I was smelling it, wearing it, tasting it, swallowing and wallowing in it. On other occasions, I stood on the open deck, exposed to the elements feeling like a Popsicle, with massive swells pressing hundreds of millions of tons of pack ice ten feet over my head every seven seconds. Then I would hear the report of the rifle, and know that I had to leave the ship and run out into the blizzard, across those formidable, moving floes, to claim and drag back a seal that often weighed more than twice as much as I did. By the looks of things turbot fishing might not pay much better than sealing, but in comparison, this was child's play. I can hang on. I can pull. I don't have to leave the ship. Nothing is worse than sealing.

Hector iced two thousand pounds of turbot in the hold. It was not all number one and there was still plenty of room down there for lots more. The plan now was to punch out the night in hopes of getting a chance to find and haul the fleet that Hector had had to tie off when the gurdy broke. Just when we had everything stowed and strapped in preparation for the battle we knew was coming, Don noticed that the gurdy was tilting towards the rail. To fix the problem Don had to weld a piece of angle iron from the rail to the gurdy for reinforcement. It was a struggle that took over two hours.

We retreated inside after that where it was everyone for himself in the galley. I ate something from the cupboard and retired to my bedroom, where Ben was at the helm. A piece of paper taped to the engine ignition read, "Do not shut off." At 11 p.m. I rolled out my sleeping bag, crawled in and braced myself for a rough night.

By 2 a.m. I was wide awake. I cursed the waves, the sea, the sky; I blasphemed the turbot and I challenged the powers that be. When I got tired of repeating the combinations of oaths, I changed their order and snarled them out again. It was the only way I knew to vent the feeling that was building up like a storm inside me. I never got a wink of sleep.

My watch commenced at 3 a.m. Speed: 1.3 knots. Winds: howling. Seas: awesome. I clung to the armrests of the commander's chair, staring out the spattered windows wondering what I was watching for. I couldn't see anything but black and green and foam in the searchlight. It was the stuff nightmares were made of. After four hundred and fifty swells burst into foam inches from my face, it was time to call Todd.

We plotted our position on the chart and I crawled back in the bag on the bench. "Unsteady as she goes 030 degrees," I said.

"Unsteady as she goes 030 degrees," he repeated, tearing open a bag of potato chips.

Thursday, September 17

BEN WAS IN THE CHAIR. JACK WAS STANDING at the chart table, holding on, looking through the spinning clear viewer when I opened my eyes to meet the day. "Fifty knots of wind out there now," Jack said, smoothly shifting his body back and forth with the roll.

"Yes, boy, every bit," Ben replied. "We'll try to find the fleet of sixty-five nets and stand by to see if we can get a chance to haul it aboard."

Icy seawater crashed at my ear and I watched the wind blow it away. Tiny ice crystals trailed down the glass, their liquid trails made haphazard by the frigid blasts. The sky looked as if somewhere to the north a huge fire burned out of control in a tire factory.

"What's for breakfast?" I asked Jack after I detected a whiff of frying food on the heat waves rising from below.

"Hector is trying to fry bologna. Go down now and he'll put on a slice for you." As I pulled my sweater over my head, I heard him say, "Make it two slices, my son, you're as skinny as a stick of gum."

I let out a chuckle as I held on to pull on my deck shoes. "My weight's all rubbed off on this bench."

〰〰〰〰〰〰〰〰〰〰〰〰〰〰〰〰

It was too miserable to stand in the lee of the wheelhouse, much less up top. From the protection of the bridge we scanned for orange on a zigzag, crash course. Just before noon, at coordinates N 60-37-760, W 60-42-307, Wayne spotted the buoys. Pitching up beside them we wallowed in the seas and confirmed that it was the northern end of the fleet of sixty-five nets. To our horror the buoys were hardly afloat. "When we shoot this fleet again, Jack, splice on another hundred fathoms of rope and another twenty-four-inch buoy," Ben ordered.

Ben figured it was best to stand by the fleet and wait to see if we could get a chance to pull it aboard. Time tumbled by. The *Styx* did her best to make the bronco ride as smooth as possible. Most of the crew slept through the following four hours. I punched some of that time holding on in the rumble seat; I spent some of the time slumped across the galley table, listlessly swaying back and forth with my head lodged on my elbow dreading the thought of pulling sixty-five nets; and I spent a little time in the washroom trying to come around. The toilet flushed every six seconds whether it needed it or not.

Ben was in the chair with both sneakers glued to the console. "Go down and tell the boys we're going to get it aboard," he ordered.

"Right away," I replied, glancing at the inclinator ball as it rolled out to thirty-two degrees.

~~~~~~

Turbot was scarce again. Number one turbot virtually nonexistent.

"Mick," Jack called from the stern pound, "come back here and pull back for a spell. Todd wants a turn on the gurdy and I'd like a spell pickin'."

I sensed by the look on Todd's face that he had no desire for my job. With the deck heaving and rolling I passed the ropes to him after he swaggered into position. As I was careening towards the pound, Jack held my arm and got my attention. I couldn't look into his eyes because of the salt and water that covered the lenses of the glasses he wore. "Don't fall overboard," he said.

I hardly acknowledged what he said until I was atop the nets in the starboard pound. Don was waiting for me to get set up. The pound area was box shaped, measuring ten feet port to starboard and eight feet fore to aft. At present the starboard pound was almost full of webbing. Don and I would be topping it up.
~~~~~~

Directly behind the pound was raging sea. Taking particular notice of the danger, I bent to grasp the headrope. The bow dipped and the stern reared. To keep from being flicked overboard, I sprawled face down atop the nets. Aware of Don watching me and waiting for me, I attempted to squat down atop the webbing and pull back. The stern plummeted. My heart came up in my throat. Spray water lashed my rubber clothes. Eagles took flight in my stomach. Instinctively, I grabbed the pound board to stop myself from being thrown out onto the deck. Noddies clucked and whirled all about. Extremely glad that I was still unhurt, I was reluctant to release my hold.

"Haul away," Jack shouted from the table. Glancing towards him I could see that the picking process was continuing. Most heads were turned in my direction.

Without saying a thing, I crouched and began to pull back. I imagined it was like being a blue-assed fly on Babe the blue ox's rump with Babe enraged and solely intent on tossing me off. When the tenth net was spread about my knees in the pound there wasn't much space left for me. Sometimes when the picking table was piled high and all hands were picking, I'd find myself up among the noddies, looking down at their sooty backs, holding on to a limp rope with my feet dangling out over the edge of the pound. We eventually tied the fleet to the rest in the port pound and the final rock clanged on the table. I wasn't sorry. Hurdy-Gurdy Man wasn't the worst job aboard after all.

Hector iced four thousand pounds of turbot, quite a lot of it suspect, and at least forty thousand pounds of garbage went out through the portal. It was obvious that we were not going to ice the seventy thousand pounds of number one turbot that we needed to keep up expectations of a fifteen-thousand-dollar payout. There were only three fleets of gear left to haul—that is, if we could find them.

Each time we stopped at different coordinates to shoot the gear out over the stern, the sea seemed to become less tolerant of us. Everything close to the rails was feather white in the night. I didn't do much other than ready a few buoys, stand back and watch Hector and Jack do the work.

After Hector tossed the last buoys into the wash and the net pounds were again empty, we gathered in the warm galley for a cup of tea and a lunch. Talk was of the sixty-mile winds that apparently were screaming towards us from the north. The plan for tomorrow was the same as for today: ride it out, hopefully haul the nets before the sea got too choppy and then get the hell out before we got blasted by the full force of the gale.

"We've been out in worse than this," Hector said soaking a slice of toast in his tea. "It was the same night the *Myers Three* sank with all hands in the Gulf of St. Lawrence. I tell you that was a rough time. The worst I ever seen it, wasn't it, Jack?"

"Yes, sir, I never seen it so bad. It was the most frightening twelve hours of my life," Jack humbly confirmed. "The aft deck was swamped. There were some nets on the bow that had to be shifted. Brian—a young fellow from home—he was a small skiver of a man, not much bigger than yourself, Mick. Anyway, this guy Brian shifted the nets. He'd take a net in each hand and run with them like they were bags of fiberglass insulation. The things you can do when things need to be done is amazing sometimes."

"I remember seeing a television program, *Land and Sea*, about that tragedy. Three brothers and a friend were lost. They found two of them, I think."

"We passed thirty miles astern of them in that squall, and that's what it was too, a squall. One that lasted all night. The storm pitched on us from out of nowhere. Before long we were battling to stay afloat," Hector went on. "We used to list out forty-five degrees, and the stabilizer arms would strike the swells constantly. I suspected that boats would sink. I was surprised, really, to hear that it was only the *Myers Three*."

Friday, September 18

WHEN JACK AWAKENED ME THE SCENE out through all forward, water-streaked windows was one of a panic-stricken ocean charging at us head-on.

A couple of hours later Ben figured it was civil enough to haul the fleet, although I never saw much of a lull in the weather. The seas crashed the same, the winds raged the same, the hull lurched the same, but all the same we started to pull the fleet aboard. Fifty percent of the sea creatures that came around were rotten. Crabs of both species infested the gear. Some reminded me of giant spiders entrapped in their own webbing. I guessed that the scent of decaying fish had attracted them. Some victims of the mono mesh were nothing but skeletons. Others burst open under the pressure and came to my hands as a mush of meat and skin. Very few rich green turbot peeled off the wheel.

The ropes parted at the twentieth net. Wayne knew the webbing was rinjacked, entangled on the bottom. He knew the ropes would break. He said so when the gurdy stalled from the strain.

~~~~~~~~~~~~~~~~~~~~~~~~~~~~~~~~~~~~~~~

Greg had finished gutting the thousand pounds of turbot the fleet had yielded. I filled three fish trays with spider crabs for a feed for the crew of the *Bakur*. When Hector was icing down the turbot in the hold, I passed down to him the trays of spider crabs. At one point when he was taking a tray from me, he looked up and said, "Hey, Mick, what's shaking?"
~~~~~~~~~~~~~~~~~~~~~~~~~~~~~~~~~~~~~~~

I glanced about before replying, "Everything, Hector. Everything." Ben had set course for the coordinates of the southern end of that fleet and we were surfing south.

At four o'clock Todd's sharp eyes detected orange off to port. We crashed over to find that two of the buoys marking the fleet were sunk. Ben decided to stay fairly close and wait for a lull. It came about an hour before sunset. "Let's get it aboard," said Ben. Like the seven blue-assed flies on bucking Babe's rump, we set to work.

During the hours that followed seawater frequently sloshed to the tops of my boots. Among the tons of garbage the monofilament entangled were four large sharks. None escaped alive. There was little conversation, but it wasn't quiet. Anytime a sixty-five-foot dragger wallows beam to, pulling a fleet of gear and its contents a mile below, on seas bashed by fifty-knot winds, there is bound to be a cacophony of noises.

The harshest and most prominent sound was that closest to me—the cracking of the ropes as the gurdy lifted the fleet. On the wind came the sounds of the sea beating at the ship. There was the sound of chain on iron, plastic striking wood. Mixed in were the sounds of the engine working, birds feasting, men toiling and dead creatures splashing. All I concentrated on, however, was my window, my balance, my timing and the rock that steadily came closer. I tried not to let the smell of rotting fish and sea sponges make me too sick. Often, the floodgates clogged with the dead. The picking table piled high with tangled webbing. Production was at a snail's pace. We had rock crabs by the hundreds, chimère by the score. Parts of the rocky bottom came round the wheel with the nets—hard coral fragments in all colors, shades, shapes and sizes. Every piece had to be picked out because even a small fragment could tangle up three or four nets as they were being set. It was a sea of heartbreak.

It was too rough to be out there working the gear. Ben knew it, but he wanted it aboard and once Wayne roped the buoys, there was no stopping until mechanical failure, fire, the weather or the parting of the ropes stopped production. Except for the noddies, and in spite of the creatures that surrounded us, the place seemed devoid of life.

Forty knots had passed through my hands before the ropes parted and the gurdy spun in another ragged end. Pulling from the southern end was our only chance of salvaging the nets left in the fleet, if we could find the buoys. But by the time we got there, it would be long past dark. As it stood, we had most of our gear and Ben decided it was time to abandon the search and set course for Port Burwell harbor. I thought about the one single buoy that floated on the last mooring and concluded that the fleet would be fishing forever. With the *Styx* shaking the seas off the starboard bow, we cleaned up our pathetic catch and iced it in the pounds. We washed up the gear and ourselves, battened down and secured the deck.

〜〜〜〜〜〜〜〜〜〜〜〜〜〜〜〜〜〜

Ten miles later Ben slowed the *Styx*. Hector had joined together the two partial fleets, forty nets in total, and shot them out. We had 148 nautical miles to go. It would take us over twenty-seven hours at the speed Ben could push the *Styx*. Any faster and the window glass or the stabilizer arm would break.

Saturday, September 19

All through the night, the dragger weathered the storm. We were in a good ship; she beat down each and every sea that reared up before her. I grew accustomed to the sound of water crashing across the windows above my head. I expected to see the foam and the spray that filled the beam of the searchlight. I wasn't a bit surprised to see the inclinator ball continually roll up to thirty degrees. At times I was apprehensive. Often I was amazed. Sometimes I felt safe enough.

My watch came with the dawn and started 98.6 nautical miles out in the Labrador Sea. Billowing, bloated snow clouds wouldn't let as much as a ray of sun peep through.

We were punching through choppy seas at 2 p.m.—when a drastic change in the ship's steerage was detected. A few minutes later the *Styx* was rolling beam to and we all knew that something was wrong with the hydraulic steering. Don told us that a bracket for the steering had snapped back in the rudder compartment. It was six hours before Don stuck his head up through the hatch opening and yelled, "Try 'er, Ben." The *Styx* reclaimed her course and Don spoke for us all when he declared, "I hope that bracket we just trigged up stands long enough to get us out of this."

At 9 p.m. we were eighty-seven nautical miles from the Button Islands and entering the outer fringes of Iceberg Alley. Speed: 5.3 knots. Winds: NW sixty knots. Temperature: -6°C. I saw enough in the searchlight beam to frighten me to death a dozen times over.

On my bed I listened as Ben hailed the *Bakur* on the set.

<hr>

"*Bakur, Bakur, Bakur. Styx. Styx.* Do you read? Over."

"*Styx, Styx.* This is the *Bakur.* Twenty-one-eighty-two, please."

"Roger."

We were fifty-three miles off the Button Islands. The turbot in our hold had to be discharged to the *Bakur* as soon as we arrived, for the *Bakur* was leaving for St. Anthony on the ebbing tide. While in port at St. Anthony, the frozen turbot they carried would be trucked to a Japanese ship tied up at Corner Brook. Fuel and water tanks would be topped up and supplies acquired. If all went according to plan, the *Bakur* would be back at anchor in Port Burwell by the time we arrived back again from the fishing grounds.

Sunday, September 20

AT 7 A.M. WE WERE FIVE MILES from the snow-glazed silhouettes of the Button Islands. It seemed as if we were getting in the lee of the land and conditions began to settle. I wasn't sorry. That's not to say that this area didn't have its own dangers. But they were more subtle and disguised. The Inukshuk watched our approach as impassively as it did our departure. It took two hours to travel up the treacherous Grey Strait to where the *Bakur* lay at anchor. Ben decided to arrange to have a new bracket for the steering, a new starter for the engine and a replacement gurdy to be sent to St. Anthony by truck. At St. Anthony they would be put onboard the *Bakur*. It was a great chance to get a few things sent from home. First on my list was lined boots. I also decided to write a letter home.

On the bow of the *Bakur* Jim stood to catch the icy bowline. It was good to see him. We were lucky to be back in.

The fish pounds were emptied in no time. The last things hoisted from the hold were the trays of red spider crabs covered in ice. I placed a tray to one side for a boil tomorrow and everyone was some happy with that. Most of the men on the *Bakur* had never seen anything like it before in their lives and a giant specimen was taken out for inspection.

"Oh, my son, you're going to taste some good later on tonight when we're steaming down the Labrador coast," Reg said to the spider crab that he held up inches from his nose.

"Well I'm sure you'll enjoy them and I hope you have a good scoff," I said.

"Thanks, my son, thanks. God bless you."

"You're welcome. God bless you, too."

The *Styx* and the *Bakur* stuck together until ice was loaded. Jack had a job for the washer and dryer. Ben was livid again when he received the tally sheet, but Kim stuck to his guns and the men dumped a lot of "inferior" turbot over the side. The final tally of "number one" was 14,500 pounds.

I scribbled a letter home telling them briefly what was happening. They could figure it out for themselves. The talk that had lured us here mentioned sixty thousand pounds of turbot a trip. In two trips we had not netted that much. But maybe our luck would change.

As I waited for the fuel tank to fill, I decided to cut out a few turbot cheeks to bring home with me. The chute on the *Bakur* that directed the reject heads and tails into the sea emptied out abreast of the starboard-side portal, where Hector usually stood when we worked the gear. Grabbing the dip net, I held it under the chute and caught three heads and tails. I then pulled in the dip net, threw the turbot heads in a tray and emptied the tails into the harbor. From the *Bakur*, Jim saw me and wondered what I was doing. As I was answering his question three large turbot heads landed in the dip net. The handle almost snapped from the sudden weight.

With a big smile on his face Jim turned towards the deck of the *Bakur* and shouted, "Come over boys and have a look at this."

Inquisitive faces peered down at me. Three turbot heads and two tails fell in the net. The heads went in the fish tub, the tails over the side. I put the net back under the chute for another head or two. The turbot men laughed.

"What are ya doin', boy?" one fellow asked in grand slang.

"Not much," I replied turning the net over to empty out a few tails and a small head.

"I see you're getting plenty of head and lots of tail," he replied, and the crowd roared in laughter. Soon the whole production line stopped and laughing faces looked down at me from everywhere. My arms absorbed the shock as twenty pounds fell into the dip net and I laboriously pulled it in, laughing along with them all. I stopped catching turbot heads when I had four trays filled.

By the time I had the ten pounds of turbot cheeks in a pile on the splitting table, our ice was loaded and we had full water and fuel tanks. I gave Jim my letter and a five-dollar bill, telling him I wanted a cold beer out of the change. I asked him to drink it for me. "No problem, pal," he replied.

"Good luck. Bon voyage. Stay out of jail," I said. The *Styx* slowly idled farther up the bay to anchorage beneath a headland about a mile from the *Bakur* and five hundred yards from the beach. Some of the crew spent the evening in their rooms, Greg spent most of it watching for targets. He shot away a box of bullets, crippling an unsuspecting gull that hovered over the bags of open garbage tossed over the side. The bird transformed from a thing of grace and beauty to a piece of "garbage" in an instant. No one asked me if I wanted a shot.

By 6 p.m. there were six of us on the bridge. Ben was in the chair, Wayne stood in the open doorway scanning the hills with binoculars, Greg and Todd were looking out, too, Doug was trying to play the guitar from my bench and I sat in the rumble seat wishing I could get ashore and be a mile away from here.

Checking in with the *Vantage,* Ben asked Jerry if there were any polar bears to be seen. Jerry told him of polar bears that had feasted on the remains of the turbot heads his crew had emptied on a knoll. One of them was massive. He ate and ate and ate. Finally, he sat down and ate. Apparently, two other bears had arrived, but they gave the giant a wide berth. They all seemed oblivious to the boat and crew who watched and taped it all. After eating what Jerry estimated to be fifty pounds of turbot heads, the giant lumbered away. That's when the other two polar bears sat in to eat. "It was better than any nature program I ever saw on television," he said.

Just then Wayne spotted a polar bear on the hillside about a thousand yards from us. Everything was white with snow, but the bear was easily discernible.

Ben keyed the mike: "Jerry, it looks like we got company. I'll call you back."

The polar bear was huge. As if he owned the place, he approached the beach.

"Todd, run down and get my rifle and some bullets. I'm going to see how fast Mr. Bear can run," Ben said, pushing open the starboard door.

Eagerly Todd ran to do his bidding. Ben placed one bullet in the magazine. Pulling the stocking cap he wore down over his ears he went outside with the rifle. Show time. Deliberately, the captain aimed and fired. The bear stopped and drew back slightly.

"Oh, so you don't want to go," Ben said, ejecting the spent shell and tossing it over the side. "Greg, pass me out another bullet."

Wayne, watching through the binoculars, said in a stone-cold tone of voice, "Go closer to him, Ben. Put it right by his big front paws."

"This one will get you movin', then, Mr. Bear," Ben said, pushing the live round into the chamber. On the sharp report of the rifle the bear abruptly spun about in its tracks and bounded away.

"Ha, ha," Ben bellowed after him, "that made you go."

"I never saw anything that big move so fast before," Wayne exclaimed in amazement.

Ben laughed again, coming inside and shaking himself to get warm. He handed Todd the rifle and told him to put it back in his room. Staring at the path the bear took I thought I could discern a blood stain on the snow, the dark red kind that the vital organs pumped. I wished I was on the *Bakur* going south tonight. I could get home from St. Anthony. I'd walk.

<hr>

That night I listened to Hector call home. "Iqaluit Coast Guard Radio, Iqaluit Coast Guard Radio. The *Styx*. The *Styx* calling Iqaluit Coast Guard Radio. Do you read, operator? Over."

Through the static, a clear voice responded and they switched frequencies. "Collect call, please, to …"

"One moment, sir, please. Yes, go ahead, please."

"Hello, this is your loving husband calling to see how you're getting on. Over."

"Oh, fine. How are you doing? Over."

"Very good, maid…"

He told of the storms and the vicious seas and the garbage and the scarcity of turbot. He inquired after the children. She sent their love. He signed off saying they'd talk again when we got in next trip with, hopefully, a full load of fish. "Loves ya, take care. Over and out."

Shortly, the operator informed Hector that the phone call had cost forty-eight dollars. In turn, Don spent seventy-five dollars, Jack spent eighty dollars and Todd's call cost one hundred and eight. It was alright for them to laugh about it. They had made the big bucks on the high seas on other trips. That night I spent thirty dollars and gave Beulah a list of things that I needed. Fortunately, things were fine at home.

Wednesday, September 23

THE RINGING OF AN ALARM STARTLED ME AWAKE. It was pitch black. I had just turned on the searchlight when Ben rushed onto the bridge. "What's going on?" he asked.

"I think we're dragging the doors," I said, focusing on the whiteness of the surf that seemed not fifty yards beyond the bow.

"Go tell the boys to get in the doors," he ordered, reaching for the starter button. The Cat didn't turn over. "Tell Don the flaming motor won't start," he called to my back.

I met Don in the galley with shirttails flying and told him about the engine. He hurried below and before long the engine revved. Ben kept the engine slow astern and Hector and Wayne reeled in the doors. When the doors clanged on the side of the hull Ben steamed the *Styx* away from the beach.

Just after dawn, I saw a polar bear swimming towards the *Styx* with its nose held high in the air. Within minutes he was right alongside the hull. I could have jumped down on his back. He saw me and without taking those cold black eyes off me, he turned abruptly and swam back towards the shore. Dreading to hear Greg coming up the ladder, I swore that he was not going to shoot that animal. Not here. Not this morning.

Climbing out of the icy water the bear paused to shake himself and look back. "Stay away from us, my fine furry friend," I said. Turning about, he sauntered away.

Sporadic small arms fire woke me up a little while later. My first thought was of the bear. Hastily I pushed back the cover and sat up to see Greg leaning out the door with the rifle to his shoulder. Getting up, I went to the chart table to see what the target was. He seemed not to notice as I stood close to his right watching him shoot at a mother murre and its chick swimming not fifty yards away. Less than a clip of bullets later, the mother was dead. The last I saw of them was the soft whites of their breasts on a sea of green and a large black and white herring gull screaming inches above the surviving chick's head.

Greg reloaded. What a way to start the day, I thought.

Minutes later, both Greg and I heard the gush of air as a whale surfaced about one hundred yards away. A mighty blast of spray mingled with the mist and slowly blew away as its entire length smoothly broke the surface before it disappeared again. Greg prepared to shoot. I hoped for the whale not to show again.

The whale did show, this time closer. Before it had dived again, Greg had stitched nine bullets somewhere in the right side of its body between the head and the tail. He quickly reloaded, but the whale didn't show again.

Fog consumed everything for the rest of that day. I turned in right after supper. The plan was to leave for the fishing grounds again at noon tomorrow. Jerry, of the *Vantage*, wasn't eager to reset his gear—that is, if he ever found it—for fear of never finding it again. Ben said we would be shooting our gear. "We're not finished with it yet," he said. I was too heartsick to care anymore.

Thursday, September 24

WHEN THE *VANTAGE* POKED HER BOW THROUGH the fog bank just after noon the *Styx* was ready to sail. By 3 p.m. we were wrapped tight in dense fog twenty miles off the Button Islands with relatively calm water and heavy swells. Ben radioed the captain of a dragger fishing farther south off Saglek Bay and we listened to tales of the caribou there. "A herd of what must have been a thousand, some with racks as big as Christmas trees, swam the fjord behind the boat a few hours ago," the voice said. When quizzed about arctic char, the voice reported seeing some in the rivers. Most everyone seemed to brighten at the news of abundant game. Ben wanted caribou. He radioed Jerry to ask him if there was some way we could get caribou hunting licenses sent up on the *Bakur*. Jerry thought that there was a good chance. Up here two animals could be taken on a single permit. The thought of a fresh caribou to bring home interested me. I didn't mind killing a caribou to eat, as I wouldn't mind the killing of a seal to eat or anything else to eat. It's when I see creatures killed and wasted or tortured that I get upset.

Contact was made and Captain Kirk replied that, if possible, he'd pick up the ten requested caribou licenses after they arrived in St. Anthony. The cost per license was seventy-five dollars. I asked Todd if he and I could go on the halves on a license.

"Can I kill it?" he asked expectantly.

"Yes, indeed you can," I replied.

"What are you going to kill it with?" Ben asked.

"Your rifle," Todd replied.

"Guess again," Ben laughed. "My rifle goes with me. I guess I'll have to shoot them all."

"I'll get my own with my .22 rifle," Greg interjected.

"You won't kill a George River caribou with that rifle, my son," Ben said to him. "You haven't got enough bullets. Those caribou are carrying around racks as big as Christmas trees, the skipper of the dragger said. If you did manage to kill a caribou, when someone asks you for a fry, you'll have to ask them if they prefer leaded or nonleaded."

Everyone but Greg laughed at that. With eyebrows lowered he went below. Chances were Ben was going to do all the hunting. We were going to be transporting five George River caribou from the tundra to the fish pounds.

"I'll cut my shells around with a knife and use them like slugs," Todd said. "I've done it before."

"Don't be worrying about the caribou," Wayne put in. "Right now we're looking for turbot. The caribou might be all gone by the time we get down there. Play us a song, Don," he said from the rumble seat. Rolling lazily port to starboard, with the fish having an easy time in moderate seas, Don didn't sound that bad to me. Maybe it's the fog in my ears, I thought. Soon Ben and Wayne went below. Todd commandeered the chair. Don strummed on for another set before retiring. Soon it was Todd and me on the bridge. He was in the mood to chitchat. I used the opportunity to ask him why he thought anyone would shoot a whale.

With what I took to be a genuine response, he said, "Dead whales make big crabs."

"I see." I sat there in the rumble chair and watched the bow break the seas to foam. Words my father had once said to me surfaced. "Don't let it torment you too much, my son. There'll always be salmon."

Sunday, September 27

AT 8 P.M., AT COORDINATES N 60-47-514, W 65-39-927, Jack threw the rock tied to the foot line of the first fleet of fishing gear into the fast-moving waters of Ungava Bay. "Rock's gone!" Fifty nets were bottom bound.

According to the chart, at 502 fathoms, this was the only deep trench in the bay within two hundred miles and it was smack in the middle of the main shipping lane of Hudson Strait, fifty nautical miles from Port Burwell harbor. Currents here surged up to seven knots. The colored depth sounder displayed a bottom that stuck up like telephone poles indicating that this was a hard place to set gear. But Ben said, "Shoot it," so shoot it we did, as if we owned the place. Then we set course for Port Burwell harbor.

The past four days and nights offshore had not been profitable. We had spent endless marrow-freezing hours on the lurching bridge searching for buoys in the foulest of conditions. And yet more hours toiling to pull gear that yielded little number one turbot but seemed full to bursting with other sea creatures, including a dozen ground sharks and what appeared to me to be squadrons of manta rays.

To add salt to the wounds, one fleet had broken free after we had battled back twenty nets. We lost fifty nets and we spent the rest of the day in a futile attempt to find the southern end.

Another fleet parted on the very next haul. Wayne knew the webbing was snagged on the bottom. The wheel spun around another ragged end and suddenly fifty nets were gone.

The fishing gear is designed, made and set in a deadly efficient way. Set like a fence across the bottom, the webbing eventually fills with sea creatures and "lies down." Crabs, the scrubbing action from contact with the seafloor and time serve eventually to consume and break down the sea creatures. When this happens the nets rise up again and fish indiscriminately. They fill up and lie down, over and over, forever. Stories have been told of draggers finding old, lost gear and the nets are filled with skeletons of every kind. As horrible as it is, it's legal and it's a common form of commercial fishing.

The forecast called for deteriorating conditions again, so the last fleet we hauled was kept aboard. We would use our remaining fleets to test the virgin waters of Ungava Bay on the way in for "our last kick at the cat."

As we headed for the sheltered waters of Ungava Bay, a pathetic eighteen thousand pounds of turbot was iced in the hold.

The crew of the *Vantage* fared even worse than we had and had spent most of the time searching for gear. The gear they did manage to find burst before they had it aboard. The eight thousand pounds they did pick from the crab-filled meshes were small. Jerry claimed that the crabs were eating the crabs. He blamed the parting of the ropes and subsequent loss of gear on the fact that the ropes were too slight. As far as he was concerned, with the vicious tides and deep grounds up here, it was the height of foolishness to set any gear with less than 5/8-inch ropes.

Ben wasn't quick to confirm Jerry's convictions. He did say that if ever they fished these waters again, he'd consider heavier ropes. In the meantime they had to make the best of what was left to make even an average return out of the trip.

Jerry scoffed at the idea of ever returning. "Ben, honest to God, if I ever can pull my gear aboard again, I'm doubtful if it will be shot out again."

"Why is that?" Ben went back.

"Because I'm doubtful if I'll ever see it again. And besides, these grounds are fished out," he claimed. "We've never fared as bad as this down off Wesleyville."

Monday, September 28

IN THE 2 A.M. DARKNESS, WE KNEW the lights that glared in Port Burwell harbor were not those of the *Bakur*. It would take the *Bakur* a few more days to complete the return trip from St. Anthony. Without knowing what ship it was, we gave her a berth of two nautical miles and steamed on up the harbor. I suggested to the boys that the name on the chart should be changed to read Port "Brrrrrrwell." It was certainly more appropriate. The temperature outside was well below freezing. A blanket of fresh snow made the hills glow, making the night look like mid-December. It was going to be a long winter.

Daylight revealed the mystery ship to be a Canadian Coast Guard ship, the *Pierre Radison*, at anchor. Ben ordered the rifles stowed away before making radio contact.

Ben received an invitation from the skipper to come aboard. So at 10 a.m. he and Don set out with offerings of fresh turbot, including two pounds of my turbot cheeks, across the three miles of choppy water that separated the two ships.

Ben and Don were aboard the CCG ship until three o'clock. I thought of keying the mike and calling the *Radison* to report the crimes against nature that I had witnessed thus far, including the fleet of nets that were, right now, illegally fishing in the shipping channel of Ungava Bay. It would be easy—all I had to do was lock both side doors and defend the bridge until the authorities arrived and put this ship under seizure. Ben would be arrested, and they'd take me back with them for my safety. I scrutinized the mike and peered down the empty staircase. All I had to do was key the mike and say, "CCG *Radison*…" But I didn't.

I was half sick and my mouth was parched when Todd came up beside me to scan for a sign of Ben and Don's return. "Are you going ashore if they gets back in time?" he asked.

"Who's going?"

"Me and Greg. I want to see the bears."

I wanted to run to the top of a hill. "Yes, boy, I'll go with you," I replied. Then, going below, I pulled on my outer clothes and my rubber pants and went down into the hold to ready the spider crabs for the *Bakur*'s blast freezer. The ship was slowly making headway up the coast of Labrador carrying new lined boots and a blanket that I hoped still smelled of home.

In less than an hour I had two new net bags, each containing fifty pounds of red spider crabs iced and ready. Then commotion above told me Ben and Don were coming back aboard.

"What a ship!" Ben exclaimed, after he climbed out of the bobbing speedboat. "And what a nice skipper. He's a true gentleman, eh, Don?"

Don agreed, unclasping his rubber clothes. Greg made ready to load the rifles and himself in the boat.

"Where you going?" Ben asked Todd.

"Ashore to Mission Harbour to take some pictures of the polar bears. Earlier, Jerry said there was three bears in there," he replied.

"Who's going with you?" Ben asked.

"Greg and Mick."

"Well, you better gas her up before you go and take my rifle with you."

Fifteen minutes later we were cutting through the waves. Greg guided us up to the slipway and we pulled the speedboat out of the water. The tide was on the ebb, gushing through the strait. We knew the less we pulled it in now the less we'd have to lug it later. When we were ashore there were no bears in sight.

But there were bear tracks all about—bear tracks that I swear would have covered a one-foot-square floor tile almost completely. All the way up the steep hill we stepped in them. At the top I stopped and said, "Boys, I'm going for a walk. See you later."

"What about the bears?" Todd asked in a surprised tone.

"If I comes afoul of any, I'll send them your way," I said, taking my first slippery step off the trail and up the steep grade away from them. Up and up I plunged with my mind focused on the bald granite summit. Nothing could stop me but a little cluster of delicate tundra flowers shivering in a hollow where no snow lay. Flopping to the ground beside them, I leaned over to inhale their fragrance before I sat up and took a look around.

Everything in sight looked the same—a monotonous marriage of a hundred shades of gray and white. The only color to be seen was of the flowers.

At the summit I could see the snow covering some areas of the tundra, while the rock faces were blown bare. The area looked like a huge creature shedding its coat. Off to the west, beneath the faint glimmer of the sun, I could discern the CCG *Radison* at anchor in the bay. In the shadowed lee of the cove, the *Styx* seemed to hide away from the CCG *Radison*'s view.

Suddenly, reports ricocheted off the bluffs and I recognized the sound of Todd's shotgun. I made my way back, meeting up with Greg, who walked alone up the path from the generator station. With apprehension and expectation saturating his voice and masking his face, he asked, "Did you hear the shots?"

"Yes," I replied. "Where's Todd?"

"I don't know."

Together we walked back to the top of the hill. When the fish plant came into view Greg and I spotted Todd standing on the roof of the building with his shotgun at ready. Upon sighting us he yelled, "Boys! Boys! Whatever you do, don't go over there! I just shot at a polar bear!"

"What?" I yelled back.

Without saying another word Todd clambered down off the roof and ran up the steep grade towards us. He almost collapsed as he stammered out the warning again.

"Don't go over there! I just shot at a polar bear!"

"Have you got any shells in that gun?" I asked him.

"Yes, five. I shot five at the bear. He was no more than thirty yards from me when I saw him. What a size! What a fright! I shouted first, but he just looked at me. I fired twice and he ran a few feet before stopping and looking back. I fired again and again and he didn't move. Then, he came towards me so I fired the last shell and ran to the roof of the plant. I couldn't launch the speedboat myself. He's just over that hill right now. Let's go back aboard," he all but pleaded.

"Do you have the safety on to that shotgun?" I asked after he stopped stammering to catch a breath. He checked the safety.

"Let's go up and see if he's still there," Greg volunteered, cradling the rifle with a lewd look in his eye.

"You go on and tell us about it later," I said, continuing on down the hill towards the plant. Todd followed in my wake. Greg hesitated for a few minutes before following.

I figured we would go aboard the *Vantage* for a cup of tea, but they wanted nothing to do with that. "Let's go see what the Inuit were doing over on the island," Todd suggested.

The tide had dropped so that Killiniq Island was no longer an island. Where the boulder bed spewed into the sea, a land bridge made it possible to walk across.

On the island, among the boulders, there stood a number of wooden crosses—a graveyard in the boulder bed. The Inuit had made a last visit with their dead before leaving for the winter. With no soil available to dig a grave, rocks were piled over the remains to prevent animals from disturbing them. Some crosses bore English names, others were adorned with Inuit markings. Todd and Greg thought they spotted ducks down in the pond. They stalked down. The sounds of gunfire from below and a cloud of squawking gulls broke the silence.

Tuesday, September 29

THAT NIGHT IT SNOWED, REMINDING ME of Christmas. The *Radison* was my Christmas tree. The moon was my star, snowflakes my tinsel. The Northern Lights did not dance. It was cold in my bedroom and I was cold all night. The thought that maybe tomorrow night I'd have an extra blanket warmed me until shortly after dawn when Jack came on the bridge. "Coming ashore, Mick? I want to go in to get some pictures of the bears," he said.

Glad to get up, I said, "Give me a few minutes to thaw and I'll go." Pushing back the bag, I sat up and looked at the morning. It was civil and clear with the winds making cat paws on the bay. Two inches of sloppy snow lay about the deck and hills. The sun was smudged out by the heavy cloud cover, but there were patches of blue about. In less than thirty minutes Jack and I were ready to go. He brought along Ben's rifle.

As soon as the old fish plant came into view, we saw the bears on the hillock in front of the *Vantage*. Jack slowed down the outboard and we idled closer. The tide was rising, surging out of the channel. At the very edge of the plant wharf watching our advance stood a giant polar bear.

I was aware of Jack standing up behind me, taking pictures. At thirty yards, I figured we were close enough and was about to tell Jack so when the engine cut out. "Oh, God, no!" he cried.

My eyes were fixed on the black eyes that were fixed on me. By the time Jack had the camera put away the fast tide had pushed the bow under the bear's nose. Paralyzed with fear that he might jump down on top of me, I didn't dare breathe. I was acutely aware of Jack frantically pulling the starter cord. The motor would only cough.

For what seemed an eternity the bear stood over me. He could have sneezed on me. I was afraid to blink. Abruptly, I felt the engine catch and Jack jam the engine into reverse. When we had backed safely away, Jack laughed and said, "Did you get a fright?"

Barely able to speak, white as a sheet, I croaked, "He could have had us." From a safe distance we watched him until he got bored and disappeared behind the buildings.

I needed a cup of tea. A double rum would have been preferred, but as far as I knew there wasn't a sup of that within hundreds of miles. Tea would suffice. "Let's go aboard the *Vantage*," I ventured.

Gerald caught our painter with a huge grin on his face. "You were close enough to him that time," he said. "All he had to do is reach down with his paw and pluck you out."

"Is the kettle boiled, Gerald? I need tea."

Jack climbed out of the speedboat. "We need new plugs for that motor," he said. "That was too close for comfort, but I got some dandy pictures."

None of the crew were in good spirits. With much of their gear lost, they had no chance now of making up a good trip. They had shipped even less turbot than we had.

The radio blared. It was Ben saying that the *Bakur* was coming around the point and we'd be off-loading right away. Without delay, Jack and I sped back to the *Styx*.

Ten minutes later we were tied to the *Bakur* and three minutes after that a crewman passed me a box with my name on it. On top was a warm blanket; just underneath was a pair of new rubber boots. There was also a letter enclosed that I left unopened in the box to read later.

The off-loading didn't take long, and the final tally wiped the smiles off every man's face. The general consensus around the galley table was that the next trip we made to the grounds could very well be our last. If the catch remained poor we wouldn't be shooting our fleets again. I figured I'd be lucky if I earned one thousand dollars on this expedition.

I read the enclosed letter later that night after everyone had retired. Thankfully, everything was well at home. Also enclosed in the envelope was a bill for $170. To think that I had not yet earned enough to pay the bill was depressing. And when the lights of the departing CCG *Radison* disappeared around the point, the place seemed black and empty.

Wednesday, September 30–
Monday, October 5

AT 5 A.M., UNDER A MOON THAT GLOWED through a veil of fog, we lifted in the doors from the floor of Port Burwell harbor and set course for the fleet of gear fishing fifty miles away in Ungava Bay. We found the buoys one mile south of the recorded coordinates. Hector iced less than a thousand pounds of number one turbot in the pound, most of it small. The nets were shredded. After we had the fleet aboard, Ben gave orders to shoot it out again before setting course for the Labrador Sea and the four fleets that were out there somewhere.

It took us until Monday, October 5, to get back some of the gear. We spent days searching for buoys in the worst weather conditions any of us had ever experienced. Night after night we plunged headlong into mountainous seas that threatened to sink us. We worked the gear when it wasn't fit to work.

The *Vantage* had salvaged some of its gear and headed back to port. Ben wanted our gear aboard at all costs.

Just before dawn on one haul Ben called me from my sleep and told me to help Hector pull in the high-fly. Drowsy and unprepared, I pulled on my rubber clothes and waited with Hector on the top deck. In my drowsiness I had forgotten to wear a pair of gloves. Ben seemed most concerned about getting the high-fly aboard without breaking the light that Hector had attached so we could find the buoys more easily.

This was the first buoy that I ever helped to pull in. When the wooden shaft with the metal reflector and flashing light reared up on the swells inches from my face, I instinctively grabbed for it. Not knowing any better I reached over the pole and held it with the wooden shaft pressed under my armpit and the metal reflector behind my back.

When the hull started its violent pitch to port the weight and strain intensified on the rope. I knew then that I was in trouble. Hector grabbed the shaft behind me and succeeded only in pressing me up against the rail. I knew I'd have to let go of the high-fly and I told him so.

Hector hollered in my ear, "Let it go!" Grinding my teeth in anticipation of the pain, I released my grip. The pole was ripped from my hands and the sharp metal whizzed past my ear before it disappeared in the darkness and spray. A roll later the light blinked in the swells one hundred yards away. On the back of my left hand hung a flap of skin that was at least two square inches.

Ben didn't swear, but he wasn't pleased. He had to get the ship in position once again. This was accomplished with a great deal of difficulty and expertise. All I did was hang on and pray to Jesus that we could get the high-fly aboard on the next attempt.

Stupidly, I grabbed the wooden shaft the same way when it again tossed up before me. When Hector's weight leaned on me I knew I was in trouble again. His face was right beside mine when I hollered, "I can't hold it, Hector. I got to let go!"

"No way!" he yelled. "It's coming aboard this time!"

I was pushing back against the pressure he was exerting on me more than I was pulling in. The hull lurched to port and I knew that if I didn't let go of the wooden shaft, I'd be crushed and slashed. Hector must have sensed the futility as well because just before he let go, he gave a growl that curled the hairs on the back of my wet neck. Feeling the pluck and letting go, I waited for the metal that I knew had to whisk by my head. And whisk it did and away it flew into the dark with another piece of my skin.

Ben was beside himself. From the open door, he yelled, "What's the matter, boys, afraid to pull it aboard?"

"There's no slack on the line!" Hector blared back at him in my defense.

"Then tell Wayne to cut it when you get a hold on it. It better come aboard this time! And don't break that light," he threatened.

The next time Hector ignored me. When the blinking pole shot up on the swell, he seized it with a vehemence that was matched only by the storm. I grabbed the pole, too, and held tight until someone below cut the rope and the cursed high-fly came in over the rail with the light still blinking. When I took off my heavy coat I found the right shoulder had a gash in it about four inches long. Too soon I heard the dreaded words, "Nets up!"

Things got even worse after that. The work involved in retrieving the fleet was spent for little reward. "A water haul," the boys called it because we pulled in nothing but water and wasted sea life.

At sea, we could jog the time for days and nights on end, but as soon as the words "Nets up!" rang through the ship, everything became a big rush. When the call came again Jack, in his race to get down to the shelter deck, decided to leap from the edge down onto the nets. The hull shuddered just as he pushed off from the wet steel plating. He toppled down on the webbing, striking his ribs on the metal partition. Balled up in the fetal position he was in agony. Don and Todd helped him hobble inside, but there wasn't much else we could do.

There wasn't any rush to bring in the turbot. We caught very little. The webbing had caught numerous round rocks like cannon balls that weighed as much as thirty pounds. It took seven hours to pick out nearly two tons of rock. Ben all but swore, "Never again will I be up here! I'll go on welfare before I come up here again!"

On another haul, the ropes parted when we had twenty nets back. We spent endless hours searching in vain for the southern end in the unrelenting seas. In the end, another fleet of deadly webbing was left to fish forever on the ocean floor and even the noddies deserted us.

~~~~~~~~~~~~~~~~~~~~~~~~~~~~~~~~~~~

On the evening of the fifth of October, with Jack still lying in his bunk, Ben called us together. We were to head for the last fleet left in Ungava Bay. If these grounds were richer we'd shoot all we had left out in the bay. If not, we'd head south. The expedition would be over.

We were heading back to Ungava Bay with 220 nets left in the pounds, a great many of them ripped up beyond repair. In the hold Hector had iced approximately seven thousand pounds of turbot.

We crossed 160 nautical miles of infuriated seas trying to swallow us every inch of the way. It was rail in, rail out all the way back.

The storm wouldn't let us pull the fleet we had in Ungava Bay, let alone set new ones. So we went straight to Port Burwell harbor. It was too rough for us to tie up to the *Bakur* to off-load. We cruised up in the far reaches of the cove and dropped anchor.

Tuesday, October 6

KIM CREDITED US WITH SIXTY-FIVE HUNDRED pounds of number one turbot. The expedition was over. While we waited for the storm to abate so we could head back to the bay to search for our lost gear, we took apart the fleets we had aboard. We pulled the nets up from the pound, untied the knots and put them back in the bags. The webbings that were ripped up beyond repair had to be cut from the headropes and footropes.
~~~~~~~~~~~~~~~~~~~~~~~~~~~~~~~~~~~

Each of these was three hundred feet long by eighteen feet deep. Once the huge pile of monofilament was freed, the ropes were coiled up and put in a bag to be stowed below. The webbing was thrown overboard.

Ben said, "Make sure you throw them well away from the rail, boys. I don't want them tangling in the blades." By the time the weather improved, we had thrown away at least fifty webbings.

The *Vantage* was moored in Mission Harbour ready to sail home. The crew had their nets pulled back and I wondered where their garbage webbings went. They had all their turbot gear taken apart and were stocking up on the salvage before they left.

At noon the *Vantage* rubbed up alongside the *Styx*. The crew said they were sailing south. Jack was feeling worse from his injuries and when Jerry suggested he get aboard with them to get medical treatment a little quicker, he readily agreed.

After the *Vantage* had slipped the lines and steamed away, Greg was most perturbed. "I thought we were going to stay together," he said as we stood about the top deck watching the ship disappear from view.

"That was the plan, but by the looks of things that's been changed," replied Ben.

"We waited for them all the way up. Now, when they got to wait on us, they desert us and go on home. A day or two for us, a day or two for them, what's the difference?" Greg growled.

"I think his crew got more to say than Jerry," Ben stated. "By the looks on their faces none of them could wait any longer to get going."

"Who's the skipper on her anyway, Jerry or the crew?" Greg asked, heaping up the tangle of monofilament in his arms and throwing it over the side. The webbing floated for a while.

After supper Don and I did the dishes. He was eager to get ashore to Mission Harbour. "That angle iron is coming aboard with me this time before we go for the fleet," he said. "We might never be back here again."

I shifted into Jack's bunk that night and slept like a baby rocked in the cradle of comfort from 9 p.m. to 8 a.m.

Wednesday, October 7

FIFTY-KNOT WINDS FLECKED WITH STINGING snow made for a miserable time on the top deck. The weather forecast for the next day or two was not good. Around noon the snow stopped for a short while and we were entertained by a fair-sized iceberg that twirled its way into Port Burwell harbor. The berg didn't just float, it spun as well. The tide was having fun enough with the hundred-thousand-ton chunk of ice. The *Bakur* had to pull up anchor and move to escape it. By the time the blizzard erupted and drove us off the top deck, the berg had gone aground about a mile away from us.

It was shortly after that we heard the mayday from the *Vantage*. Apparently Jerry had sought refuge from the storm in a bay about one hundred miles down the coast near Cape Kakkiviak. A cable had snarled in the blades and the ship was in danger of driving ashore. An Iqaluit Coast Guard operator responded and we listened as Jerry told the operator of his dire straits. Anxiously we waited for news.

"There you go now. That's what they gets for taking off and leaving us," Greg stated crudely.

"Yes, by the sound of Jerry, he's some sorry he's not anchored in Mission Harbour right now," Ben added.

About an hour later Jerry informed the operator that his crew had tied to ropes everything that was stowed in the hold and anything that wasn't welded to the deck. They had then thrown everything overboard in the hopes that something would catch on the bottom and hold them. One hundred yards from disaster the *Vantage* had stopped dragging its anchor and at present was holding her own.

The operator requested assistance from any ships in the area. Ben responded, gave the operator our position and stated that the *Styx* would steam to assist the *Vantage* if the operator could guarantee compensation for the fleet of nets we were leaving behind. The operator could not guarantee this, so we stayed put. Finally it was arranged that the MV *Tellios,* a seismographic ship working eighty miles out in the Labrador Sea, would steam to their assistance.

The storm raged all that evening and into the night. I spent most of my time stretched out in Jack's bunk reading a book, waiting for news about the *Vantage.* At 10 p.m. we heard that the *Vantage* was safely tied to the MV *Tellios.* The *Tellios* would stand by until divers could be flown down from Iqaluit to untangle the cable. The charge was fifty dollars per hour.

At the same time Ben received notice that the *Bakur* had been called back to Halifax by the ship's owners. It just was not profitable having them here waiting on a fleet of gear that we all suspected was lost.

Around 10 p.m., after refueling, we slipped away from the *Bakur* for the last time.

Thursday, October 8

ALONE ON ANCHOR WATCH I WATCHED the *Bakur* steam out of the harbor on the radar. By 2:30 a.m. it was just the *Styx* and the iceberg. It was an eerie feeling to be left in such a desolate, inhospitable place. The forecast was for diminishing winds in the bay. Ben figured we'd be sailing for the gear around 6 a.m. It was still cold; the temperature hovered around -15°C.

At noon, after a halfhearted search for the gear in Ungava Bay, we gave up. It seemed the vicious tides had stolen them away or a passing ship had dragged them off.

Ben set course for home. I didn't hear one complaint from anyone. So we departed the hostile environment, leaving a great deal of our gear still fishing.

Ben still had caribou on his mind, license or no. He'd kill the caribou on the way along and send the *Vantage* into Makkovik to pick up the licenses while we waited offshore. Then we'd tag the meat and all would be legal. I no longer cared one way or the other. This was the way things went on this ship.

From the top deck we watched Cape Chidley pass by one mile off to starboard shrouded in fog, glazed in ice and snow. At 8 p.m. we were abeam and fifteen miles off the twin rounded summits of Cape Kakkiviak, where Jerry and the *Tellios* were located. Icebergs, big and small, infested the seas all around us.

Ben had his sights set on Saglek Bay for the caribou. Jerry would meet up with us there after divers freed them.

"Security, security, security," the radio crackled. We were in for another blow. At 9:40 p.m. we were at coordinates N 59-47-126, W 63-21-492, experiencing moderate northeast winds at thirty-five to forty-five knots, eighty-five nautical miles north of Saglek. Hopefully we'd be safely in the fjord before the storm pitched.

Friday, October 9

AT DAWN WE LEFT THE SWELLS AND ENTERED the fjord. We were now beneath the headlands I had seen fifty miles out to sea. They towered over us. From the water's edge they went straight up for two thousand feet. Snow covered the highest granite summits and veined the sheer faces. Slowly and steadily we passed by to find even more panoramic views of the mighty Torngats, untamed, uninhabited and unspoiled.

The fjord narrowed as we cruised deeper into its quiet recesses. Don and Wayne came on the bridge and both commented on how beautiful and picturesque the place was. As I listened to them I wondered how anyone who could appreciate this beauty and serenity could still wreak such violence and cruelty on any creature that swam, crawled, walked or flew.

At noon we dropped the doors about a half-mile from where a small brook flowed into the bay. On the beach huddled two buildings, and two boats were pulled up and overturned well above the high-water mark. I could sense the excitement and expectations of the crew as they hurried to launch the speedboat to get ashore. All but Hector boarded the small boat, armed to the teeth with rifles and shotguns, rods and reels. I felt a pang of pity already for any living creature that we happened to encounter.

The first thing we saw were the tracks of two wolves in the snow where we pulled up the speedboat. All guns were loaded and ready. We crossed the small stream and trekked over the tundra up the narrow gorge through which the stream cut. About a mile from the beach, atop a snow-covered knoll peppered with fox tracks, we stopped to survey the terrain for anything alive. A larger river flowed into another cove, forming a delta of twisting riverbeds lined on both banks with gnarled spruce and alder. Todd thought he saw some ducks. Leaving me with the rod, he stalked down to investigate. Don, Greg and Wayne walked towards a waterfall that we could see about a mile inland. Ben stayed by me scanning the terrain with binoculars for something to shoot.

It was a beautiful day, not at all cold, and although the sun did not shine directly on us, it did shine on some of the lofty peaks. I was content to just sit and take it all in when Todd yelled from the delta, "Boys, there's char down here. Bring down my rod!"

The tide was out and a school of maybe fifty were stranded in the shallow waters of the stream, a sandbar blocking their escape.

"Just look at 'em!" Todd exclaimed. "Just look at the size of them!"

When I saw the fish I noticed that they were big but thin. "They're spawning," I said. "They're no good to eat, they're all spawned out!"

"I don't care about that," he replied excitedly. "Pass here my rod."

Reluctantly I passed it to him and he put his shotgun aside. He untied the heavy lure, detached the large three-barbed hook and tied it on the end of his spider wire. The fish were ten feet from him, trying to hide beneath an overhang in the bank. He cast his hook and plucked up viciously. The reel snarled as the startled char charged downstream towards the sandbar that blocked their escape. Catching one, Todd dragged it towards him. He was all smiles when he held up the torpedo-shaped char by the gills for Ben and me to see. "What a fish!" he exclaimed with a gleam in his eye.

"It would be a much finer fish if it wasn't spawned out," I said.

He never acknowledged my comment. Grabbing a rock he bashed the life out of it before throwing it on the sandbar. Then I heard the sound of Ben's reel snarling out line. He jigged into one almost immediately. As the school diminished in number the char became more frantic. In their panic to escape a couple drove themselves high and dry. Ben booted them farther ashore and rushed to grab and kill them.

"Don, Don," Todd yelled, "come over here. This is where the char are. Yahoo!" he bellowed as he ripped into another. The last pitiful few sought refuge from the hooks underneath the overhanging banks. With the tip of his expensive rod, Todd poked around until the unfortunate fish scurried out in the open. My mouth went dry. I left them and returned to the snowy knoll where the fox tracks were. "It could be worse," I thought. "At least they lived long enough to spawn."

Ben spotted movement high up in the heights and as he passed me by he told me to come with him to investigate. Ascending the steep grade, Ben's excitement rose as we spotted fresh caribou tracks. From the rocky summit I could see Todd and Don down in the delta hunting down the char without mercy. I spotted Greg off by himself over by the waterfalls. The height gave us a spectacular view of our ship of death peacefully at anchor in the fjord. Ben scrutinized the tundra for caribou. I looked as well, but my mind was made up. As much as I'd like to have one for the winter, I wouldn't tell him if I saw a herd of ten thousand.

After about an hour, I could see that the jigging spree was over and Todd and Don were bringing their catch up to the knoll. Ben told me to go back down to where they were and help them take the char back to the ship. I was glad to be away from Ben, but at the same time I wasn't eager to be with the others. But down I went.

I guessed they caught about 130 pounds of char and had most of them piled on the knoll. Don was on his way back to the beach with his. Todd was down by the stream retrieving the remaining ones from the sandbar. "By Jesus, you won't be getting them all!" I said out loud. Picking out three of the biggest ones, I buried them in the snow and made like there was nothing there. A fox or a wolf could have a feed.

As Todd and I walked back we heard the sound of the outboard from a small rise one-quarter mile from the beach. It was Greg speeding back to the ship alone. Ben was exiting the larger wooden building and Don was sitting on a rock by the small stream. We sat down beside him and decided to clean the catch. Ben came up alongside and sat down. Wayne was nowhere to be seen.

Suddenly Ben spotted a head in the cove about two hundred yards away. "That's a sea otter!" he exclaimed in a whisper. "Todd, is there any shells in your gun?"

"Yes," he replied, "she's fully loaded."

Without further ado, he snatched up the shotgun and started to creep around the cove, stalking the unsuspecting creature that swam and bobbed and played in the sea. When it dived, Ben would run for a short ways, then hide behind a rock while the otter showed. Eventually he was within range and hid down until the animal surfaced. We all watched him raise the gun and aim it at the back of the black head thirty yards away. Boom! sounded the gun, followed by a blast of lead that sprayed the head just before it disappeared. When the animal showed again it was jerking around in pain. Boom! sounded the gun again and the animal floated lifelessly. Ben broke cover and ran towards it. "Mick!" he bellowed.

"What?" I answered.

"Bring over Todd's rod. I need it to hook it in."

A few decibels lower than the babbling of the brook, I picked up the rod and swore silently to myself. "What is it you got killed?" I asked upon approach.

"It's a seal, not a sea otter" he replied. "Fresh flipper tomorrow," he proclaimed, taking the Davy Crockett stance. "Give me your knife," he said.

He split it open and cut out the flippers, tossing them on the beach. "Help me drag the carcass up past the high-water mark," he said, bending down and grabbing it by the rear flippers.

"Why?" I asked.

"Because I'll get a shot at a fox or a wolf tomorrow morning," he said. I helped him drag the mutilated corpse, and we returned to Todd and Don. He carried the flippers, I toted the gun and the rod.

Hector appeared on the bow and Ben hailed him ashore. Then he became concerned about Wayne. Don said the last time he saw him, he was walking through a gorge between the mountains over by the waterfalls. That was hours ago. It was now four o'clock and time for him to be back. "It's not sensible," Ben said, "to be walking around this wild country alone with nothing but a shotgun. Only a jerk would do that. Is that the same way the wolves went, Don?" he asked, scanning the rolling open tundra.

"Yes, the same way," Don answered, following his worried gaze.

"Well, if he's not back in an hour or so you'll have to go look for him," he said. "Put the fish in the boat, boys, and me and Hector will go back aboard."

We spent most of the hour looking around the larger of the two wooden buildings. It was well stocked with all the necessities for a good life, including a few adult magazines.

"Ohhh! Don't be looking at that stuff," Don said, looking over my shoulder when I unfolded the center spread atop the table.

"What! What's wrong with that, Don?" I said, pulling out a chair and sitting down.

Todd came over. "What are you looking at, boys?" he asked, with his beady eyes feasting on the picture.

"What does it look like?" I asked, holding it up. "Under that top mattress there's another one. Go in and bring it out."

"Nooo, I can't go looking at that stuff," he said, turning towards the open door.

"Why? What's wrong with that, old man?"

"Nooo, I can't go looking at that stuff," he repeated.

Don followed him out saying, "Come on, Wayne!" in an agitated tone of voice.

"I'm bringing this aboard for Hector," I said, prodding them even further.

Don turned around, stomped back to get another good eyeful and, without lifting his eyes from the picture, said in a threatening tone, "If Ben finds out that's aboard, he'll put you off in the speedboat."

I laughed and closed the magazine. He turned and walked outside. On one wall about a dozen names and addresses were written. Picking up a pencil I wrote my name and the date. Outside, we hung around the front step watching the vista for some sign of the "jerk." I dreaded the thought of going up in those mountains at this time of the evening. Already the shadows of the heights were darkening the valley in spite of the snow. The longer I looked without seeing Wayne, the less eager I was to go. Don was the one finally to say the dreaded words, "Let's go find him, boys."

Walking back across the barrens, along by the char I hid, we saw human tracks atop the two wolf tracks heading up the steep slope. We stopped and called. Only our echo came back to our ears.

"Well, boys," I said, "I'll bet you that those two wolves know we're here."

Todd wouldn't or couldn't go any farther. Don asked if I'd go on and I said, "I think any jerk foolish enough to go alone into the unknown following two wolves, not telling anyone where he was going or when he'd be back, deserves a night out to get his head straight."

"I agree," Don said, "but we got to find him."

With a great degree of apprehension, I replied, "Lead on, Don, lead on."

Turning to Todd, he said, "You wait here and if Wayne shows, call out."

Todd agreed and up the slippery slope we started following the tracks. The grade became steeper and more slippery, and it was getting darker. We stopped on a small plateau, the summit another five hundred yards above. Here the tracks separated. Wayne went left, the wolves right. Don made a few more bawls. No reply. I was slipping around quite a bit getting this far. Most of the time I used my hands to help me up the greasy grades and over and around the rocky crags and glacier droppings. Below us the shadows had captured the valley all the way to the beach.

I was becoming more and more concerned. I didn't want to slip and skid three hundred feet down the face of this granite mountain. "How much farther are you going, Don?" I asked, inhaling the crispy air deep into my hard-working lungs and exhaling it like smoke.

He pointed to the lip of the next highest plateau, a hundred yards ahead and up. "I figure we'll go to that lip. If we don't find him then, we'll go back."

"I'll wait for you here," I said, sitting on a bare cold boulder.

Don walked away and I was left alone. At the top of the lip he hollered several times. Nothing but his echo bounced back. "To hell with the jerk, Don!" I said to the boulder. "He's a big man that gives it to whales in the head. He can take care of himself. Come on! Let's get the hell down out of this while we have the chance!"

Don walked back down the grade in the gloom of the dusk, the lights of the *Styx* blazing across the distance. Before long we heard Todd shouting, "Boys, come on. Wayne's out!" Farther up the gorge and a lot closer to the boat than Todd was, I could vaguely discern Wayne walking near the hillock where I buried the char. By the time we caught up to Todd, Wayne was on the beach.

By the time we arrived at the beach Wayne had been sitting in the darkness for twenty minutes. The valley was barely discernible. Don walked right up to him and said, "Where were you, Wayne?"

"I was up on the mountain hunting partridge," he said from his seat by the stream. "Come here 'til I shows ya." Pulling his pack up beside him, he proudly opened the flap and counted eight dead white partridge, which he spread out on the sand. "I was hunting them all day. There was nine of 'em. One got away, but not without losing a few feathers. When it started to get dark, I gave up and came out."

"You shouldn't be going off by yourself," Don said seriously.

"I know, boy," he replied, stuffing them back in his bag. "But I got the birds though, didn't I?"

Hector pulled up on the beach with the speedboat and we stood up. Wayne never as much as acknowledged the fact that we spent the last two hours tromping the mountains and dales looking for him. The jerk.

On the way back to the boat, I sat on the thwart right in front of him. I hawked loose a small piece of the lump that stuck to the back of my throat and spit it overboard right in front of him.

The smell of fried char greeted us as we climbed aboard. Six of the scrawny fish were lying on the picking table. Not in the least bit hungry for jigged char, I opted for caffeine.

After most of the crew had retired to their berths to sleep off supper, Hector and I did the dishes. "Those fish never had a chance," I said, tying tight the garbage bag knot.

"Did they leave any?"

"I don't think so."

Without thinking anything of it I took the two garbage bags outside, opened the hatch cover and tossed them down on top of the melting ice in the center pound. Through the portal I could see the moon. It drew me to the rail. Then an intense psychological low stalled over my soul. I was aware only of gloom even though I was bathed in the brilliant moonbeams that blazed down on me. Don's words echoed inside my head: "If Ben finds out that's aboard, he'll put you off in the speedboat."

"Yeah! He thinks he will. He'd need all this crew to do it and the crew of the *Vantage*, too," I said to the dead char.

~~~~~~

Ben never had his shot at the wolf the next morning. While talking to Jerry on the set that evening, we were informed that divers had arrived just before dark and in only a couple of minutes had the cable removed. Currently the *Vantage* was cruising down the coast. Jack wanted to come aboard again. We would rendezvous later. Ben wanted caribou. He wasn't eager to go home. "We're up here and chances are we might never be up here again. Why not take our time and look around?"

The forecast called for diminishing northerlies, offering a good time surfing south. At midnight we pulled in the doors and left Saglek Bay. I sat in the rumble seat for a while and watched the towering headlands silently pass by. With the first swells, I went below and crawled in to enjoy my last night in a comfortable bunk. Tomorrow night I'd be back on the bench again. All occupants were asleep.

Saturday, October 10

WE ENTERED THE FJORD NORTH OF HEBRON to make the human transfer at 7 a.m. Here the awesome Torngats rose from the sea. When we tied the *Vantage* broadside, Jerry's face startled me. He looked haggard and beaten.

In the galley the discussion was about the plans. Jerry wanted to go directly home, as did the rest of his crew. Ben wanted caribou and his crew didn't mind staying. "What about licenses, Ben?" Jerry asked. "You can't risk this one with illegal meat! If you're caught this boat is gone!"
~~~~~~

"There's no meat aboard yet," Ben countered. "What's the rush to get home, anyway? Are ya homesick or what? We're up here, so why not see a bit of the country? We might never be up here again; why not have a look around?"

"I say we go on home," Jerry decisively stated.

"What if you went down to Makkovik and picked up the licenses and came back?"

"I'm not doing that, Ben! That's two days' steam. No, I'm not doing that! When I head down, I'm not coming back!"

"Well, you please yourself. I'm going to take my time and cruise home. What if it takes another day or two. What odds!"

Before we cast off I grabbed the chance to speak to Ronny, a crewman on the *Vantage*. He looked old and worn, his long face unshaven, his hair unkempt. "Mick," he said with what I took to be true conviction, "if I knew I could swim from here to the wharf in the harbor I'd dive in right now."

"That bad, is it?"

"Bad is not the word for this. This is the worst! The worst!"

With Jack again tucked away in his bunk and me re-established in mine, we spent the day cruising the fjord watching for wildlife. The *Vantage* followed about a mile behind. After dinner, while I was sweeping up the galley, the door burst open and Ben rushed in. At first I thought there was an emergency. He went directly to his room and promptly reappeared with his rifle. "What's going on?" I asked.

"There's a bear in there," he said without breaking his stride. Tossing the broom in the corner, I followed him up the steps. In the cleavage of two pert, round peaks, I saw the black bear foraging in the landwash. He had no idea we were near. Wayne slacked the throttle and we coasted to idle. Then the stern door dropped with a loud, resounding clang. The bear heard it and turned to look at us. In a stretch gallop that did not slacken, he plunged up the steep grade without looking back.

"You can't go!" Wayne exclaimed.

"No, you can't," Ben agreed. We watched him run up the steep face, go over the crest and disappear from view. Wayne put the transmission ahead and we continued our excursion.

The next bear wasn't so lucky. Todd spotted him on the beach about a mile ahead. Ben slowed the engine and ordered the speedboat launched. Within a few quiet minutes the unsuspecting black bear was being stalked by Todd, Ben and Greg. From the top deck I watched them very slowly and quietly close the distance, with Ben ready in the bow. Resting his rifle atop a life jacket, he took sight and fired. The bear dropped in its tracks as the report of the rifle echoed off the granite faces and ricocheted down the canyons. Greg gunned the engine and a few moments later they were standing over it.

We drifted in the cat paws waiting for them to do their dastardly deed. Soon they sped back and passed up the bear skin to Don. It was a small bear, maybe two years out on its own. Ben was the hero. "One shot. One shot dropped him in his tracks. He didn't know we were in the world and now he never will," he proclaimed. Todd stretched the skin out on the picking table. "Take in the boat now, boys." By the time we resumed our cruise out of the fjord, Todd had the skin salted down and stowed in the hold.

At 5 p.m., at coordinates N 58-12-304, W 62-36-735, we dropped our doors in the lee of Dog Island, about a mile from the huge church in Hebron. Besides the church, seven small, dilapidated wooden shacks made up what was left of the once thriving community. Without delay we launched the speedboat and all but Hector, Jack and me went ashore with guns and rods, returning just before dark. I had no interest in going with them. I had seen enough killing. I swore the next time I stepped ashore, there'd be no back aboard. I turned in on my bench, taking comfort in knowing that my time among them was getting short. The *Vantage* waited one-quarter mile away.

Sunday, October 11

WE GOT UNDERWAY AT 7 A.M. CRUISING through the tickle between Kingmirtak Island and the Harp Peninsula. In Okak Bay grew the first trees—orange juniper and stunted spruce—and there was caribou. In the hundreds, they were all about the tundra, on the beaches and swimming in the water. Everyone came up to see. Ben wanted to stop. "Look at 'em in there!" he exclaimed time and time again. He radioed Jerry who was about a mile astern and a mile to port, who told him not to stop. Ben was frantic.

By 5 p.m. we were cruising down the coast in the lee of the Torngats, making a steady speed of 9.4 knots and leaving all the caribou safely behind. The wind and friendly whitecaps struck the starboard with little or no effect other than a little spider's piss softly spraying the windows about twice a minute. The Tikkerasuk Peninsula slowly passed abeam, twenty miles away. We were experiencing a good time along. I spent a comfortable night on the bench. Thoughts of home prevailed in my mind most of the night. I would soon be back, just as penny-short and desperate as before I left. The talk aboard the ship now was of crab. They had two more trips to make. As soon as they got in, the *Styx* would be made ready. "Moneypots" the boys called the crab pots. Dead whales make big crabs. I knew it had to be more lucrative than turbot and sealing.

Monday, October 12

MY WATCH AT 1 A.M. IS ONE I'LL NEVER FORGET. It wasn't a bad night coming down Iceberg Alley thirty miles off the coast. The southwesterly breeze off Cape Mugford gently foamed the ten-foot swells. The fish were swinging in the air, dangling from the extended stabilizers. Fourteen bergs blipped on the radar screen. Watching the beam, I first detected a few pieces of telltale ice rubble on the rising face of the oncoming swell forty yards ahead. My eyes fixed on the spot as the swell crested and foamed to reveal a chunk of ice. The beam confirmed that it was a growler when the light reflected off it back at my startled face.

The hull softly listed out to starboard and I lost sight of it. Before I could react to punch Otto's manual button, the hull listed back to port. Instead of taking emergency measures and evasive action, I watched for the growler. The greenish chunk of certain devastation showed briefly before it disappeared right beside the bow. Instinctively, I held on with both hands to absorb the shock, tightening my body and grinding my teeth when I thought the hull would strike. Nothing happened. I relaxed a little when I knew we had passed it, figuring if the hull had had another coat of paint, we would have struck. Looking ahead for other pieces I saw nothing. The *Vantage* was a mile astern, well to port of the growler. I thought to call but decided not to. My heart was racing. I pushed open the top half of the starboard door and lit a cigarette. When Todd came up to relieve me, I told him about the growler and he asked me to double another watch with him. I don't think I would have slept anyway.

We spent most of the favorable day on the top deck pulling back nets and discarding the garbage over the rail. I'd watch the webbing float in the wake for a short spell before it disappeared. After Greg had discarded about a dozen, I could hold my tongue no longer. "Boys, that don't make any sense to me," I said.

All the crew but Wayne and Ben stood around me with sharp knives that they used to cut the string that tied the webbing to the rope frame.

"What makes no sense to you?" Don asked.

"Tossing those webbings overboard. Why can't we keep them in the hold until we get home? We won't have all of them pulled back by the time we get in. I'm sure you'll have to go to the dump with some. Why not take them all?"

"Dump 'em now," Greg said. "Garbage is garbage."

"What about everything that could get caught up and die in them for the next twenty-five years? The salmon stocks will soon be coming this way heading for the rivers to spawn. What about whales and porpoises and seals and birds?" I said, trying to keep my voice even and calm.

"What about it?" Greg asked, his eyes riveted on the section of net he held in his hands.

"What about it! You're a fisherman, for God's sake! Don't you care about it?"

"We don't have a license to catch whales, or porpoise or salmon," he replied. "As for seals, they're dirt anyway."

I didn't say anything else. Hector started to sing a gospel song, Don asked Todd what he was going to do when he got home, Greg went to the rail to take a leak and I hawked loose a piece of the lump of disgust from my throat and spit it on the deck. The headlands of the rugged snow-covered Torngat Mountains fell slowly astern. By the time we called it a day twenty-four monofilament webbings and a deep freeze were over the rail, all well clear of the hull.

Tuesday, October 13

JACK AND I DOUBLED ON WATCH FROM 3 to 5 a.m. We were abeam *Black Tickle* and it was snowing by the reeves. Our course cut through the drift at a steady speed of 8.5 knots, 183 nautical miles, 21 hours, 28 minutes from home port. The seas about us were calm, the night that cloaked us was black as pitch. The

Vantage bleeped on the radar four miles astern. Jack's ankle and ribs still hurt, but he was tired of lying around and could hobble enough to do his watch. He told me he was glad to be aboard after the harrowing experience in the fjord. I knew by the look on his face that he meant it. "I wouldn't want to work onboard that one," he said.

At 9 a.m. we were abeam of Belle Isle; the Labrador coast had fallen astern. The weather was civil, and the snow turned to rain, making for a miserable time on the aft deck hauling back and discarding nets. If all went well we'd be in port by midnight.

At 2:15 p.m. we had our first shrouded glimpse of Cape Bauld. "God bless the Rock," Hector said. As cold and barren and bleak as the cape looked in the fog and mist, it made me feel a lot better.

By 6 p.m. we were approaching the Grey Islands. It was still foggy, but the swells were soft and smooth. Murres livened up the waters; companies of them, the chicks now almost as big as their mothers. Greg and Todd fired off the last of their ammo, making whatever came within shot pay with their very lives. I couldn't wait for this to be over. I couldn't wait to tell.

Wednesday, October 14

AROUND MIDNIGHT THE LIGHTS OF La Scie harbor were shining there for me. Wayne phoned home and informed his wife that he'd be driving home after we arrived. I asked for a lift.

There was quite a reception for us on the wharf. Men, women, children and grandchildren waited eagerly for their heroes. There were hugs and kisses almost all around. Wayne had the truck pulled alongside the ship and with my bags packed and loaded I sat waiting for him, feeling happier than I had for a long time. My own bed was but three and one-half hours away. The ride home was relatively conversationless and uneventful.

When I finally closed the truck door, unpacked my gear and stood in my driveway watching Wayne pull away, I was greatly relieved. It was finally over. I had endured. The kids were excited to have me home. An hour later, after weeks on the hard bench, I sat on my side of the bed, almost ready to lie back.

Woefully, I figured that, after deductions, my net gain was near nil. I decided to keep that a secret for now. Just as my tired neck was about to touch the fresh clean pillowcase, the thought of the $170-care-package bill crossed my mind.

Glossary

Abeam: at right angles to a ship's keel.

Aft: close to or towards the stern of a ship.

Beam to: waves striking on the broadside of a ship.

Bow: the front part of a ship.

Bulkhead: a wall inside a ship that creates a watertight compartment.

Chimère: common name (French) for the deep water, bottom-feeding fish, chimaera.

Coleman: the sides of the hatch.

Fish: devices used to stabilize a ship at sea.

Fisherman's bend: type of knot used to tie gill nets together.

Fore: the front part of a ship.

Forecastle: area on a ship immediately aft of the bow.

Gill nets: nets used to catch fish by the gills.

Growlers: fragments of icebergs.

Gunwale: the upper edge of the side of a ship.

Gurdy: apparatus used to pull fishing gear from the seafloor.

Head: the bathroom on a ship.

Hold: that area of the ship used to store the catch.

Hull: the hollow, lowermost portion of a ship.

Lee: the side of a ship that is sheltered from the wind.

Otter boards: apparatus used to keep nets fishing while they are being dragged.

Port: the left-hand side (looking forward) of a ship.

Portal: an opening in the side of a ship through which gear is pulled.

Porthole: a window in a ship.

Pounds: areas bounded by boards used to retain fish.

Share man: a crewman who receives a share of the catch.

Shelter deck: work area on a ship enclosed by three walls.

Stanchion: an upright support.

Starboard: the right-hand side (looking forward) of a ship.

Stem: the forward part of a ship.

Stern: the back part of a ship.

Top deck: area above the shelter deck, aft of the wheelhouse.

Wheelhouse: the command center of a ship.